collectors'
PAPERWEIGHTS

collectors'
PAPERWEIGHTS
*price guide
and catalogue*

by Lawrence H. Selman

PAPERWEIGHT PRESS
Santa Cruz, California

Dear Collector,

It is with great pleasure that we present our new catalogue. It offers the largest selection of quality antique and contemporary paperweights available to collectors today. It also provides an introduction to the exciting and challenging world of paper-weight collecting.

In addition to photographs and descriptions of over 400 paperweights and related objects, this edition offers collectors a history of paperweights and how they are made; detailed material about individual glass factories and studio artists; and information on collecting, determining authenticity and paperweight restoration. Complete reference listings of contemporary sulphides, Baccarat Gridel silhouette weights, and an extensive glossary of paperweight terminology are also included.

We are pleased to introduce several new paperweight artists in this edition. These new artists, along with the many other well-known contemporary glass artists working today, are contributing greatly to the future of paperweights. Their innovative ideas and approaches to design and technique add vitality and diversity to the art.

Over the past eighteen years we have watched interest and appreciation for paper-weights grow by leaps and bounds. This growth can be attributed to the fact that more and more people are aware of the beauty and unique qualities of these objects, and that both antique and contemporary weights have proven to be excellent investments. Hundreds of collectors have found paperweights—their history, identification and acquisition—to be a fascinating and rewarding pursuit.

We hope you will enjoy using this catalogue as a reference tool as well as a means of improving and developing your collection. Please feel free to call us with your questions or comments. We are always available to help you.

Sincerely,
Lawrence H. Selman

TABLE OF CONTENTS

COLLECTING PAPERWEIGHTS

EVER SINCE GLASS paperweights were first created by European glass factories in the 1840s, these brilliant works of art have been valued and collected. A number of well-known personalities, including Queen Victoria, Colette, King Farouk, Truman Capote, and Eva Peron, were serious paperweight collectors. Many prominent museums such as the Smithsonian Institution, the Metropolitan Museum of Art, the Victoria and Albert Museum, the Corning Museum of Glass, the Art Institute of Chicago, and the Bergstrom Museum maintain paperweight collections.

Paperweights offer the collector countless hours of discovery and enjoyment as well as an excellent investment opportunity. While the market for many other types of glass, such as American art glass and French cameo glass, has experienced steep ups and downs based on fad and fashion, the antique and contemporary paperweight market has shown a steady rise in value. A few very special pieces have skyrocketed in price within a short time. The most dramatic example is the much-publicized Pantin silkworm weight purchased in the late 1920s for $59 which sold in 1984 for $143,000!

There are many different approaches to paperweight collecting. Collections can be built on contemporary annual editions from Baccarat, Saint Louis or Perthshire; the exciting and innovative pieces by American studio artists; or select antique finds. Collecting sulphides offers a unique way to enjoy the beauty of paperweights while commemorating and appreciating historical events and personalities. Many collections are based on themes such as a specific maker, certain types of flowers, or particular design motifs. No matter what approach the collector takes, the key to developing a good collection is knowledge and a concern for quality and beauty rather than quantity.

Determining Authenticity

There are many complex and varying factors which determine the value and desirability of a particular paperweight. Where and when a piece was produced, the design, workmanship, condition, and rarity must all be considered. The most reliable way to determine the provenance and authenticity of a weight is to consult an expert. The next best way is to carefully research the weight in question by studying as many reference sources as are available. It is important to do this before purchasing the weight, as there are many high-priced, unauthenticated "antiques" on the market today.

Collectors can become familiar with paperweights and their history through a number of excellent books on the subject and by examining weights first-hand in museums, galleries, and private collections. Also, the Paperweight Collectors' Association (founded in 1954) publishes an annual bulletin containing articles about rare paperweights, special collections, conferences, artists, and factories.

Please feel free to send us a photo of a weight you are considering for purchase. We will notify you by return mail if it is worth the asking price and if it is indeed what it is represented to be.

L. H. Selman Ltd.

Active in the paperweight field since 1968, L. H. Selman Ltd. offers collectors the finest selection of antique and contemporary paperweights available on the market today. The paperweights shown in this catalogue demonstrate the quality and variety we offer our clients on a regular basis.

In 1975 we started Paperweight Press, which publishes books and information about paperweights, promotes historical research in the field, and documents contemporary paperweight artists and trends. One of our publications, *Paperweight News*, is a quarterly newsletter which provides collectors with a range of articles and information about paperweights.

We also provide professional appraisals for individual collectors, businesses, corporations, and museums. Some of the collections we have appraised include: the Arthur Rubloff collection of over 1100 weights, which is now a permanent exhibit at the Art Institute of Chicago; the Doheny Collection in Camarillo, California; the Fowler Collection in Los Angeles; and many other public and private collections.

Our staff is available to answer questions, advise on collecting, and to send any information you may require. We look forward to helping you build an outstanding paperweight collection.

A HISTORY OF
PAPERWEIGHT
MAKING

A HISTORY OF
PAPERWEIGHT MAKING

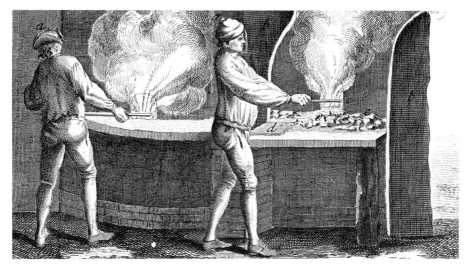

THE EARLIEST GLASS paperweights, sulphides, were sculpted ceramic cameos completely encased in crystal. First developed during the 1750s in France, sulphides were later refined and perfected in England by Apsley Pellatt, who took out a patent on the technique in 1819. Glass encrustations, which often commemorated important individuals and historic events, were extremely popular throughout the nineteenth century. In addition to paperweights, they were used to ornament a variety of glass objects including decanters, perfume bottles, seals, candlesticks, buttons, and jewelry.

There is little definitive information available as to when French glass factories first produced millefiori paperweights, but it is believed that the major inspiration came from the Exhibition of Austrian Industry held in Vienna in 1845. It was there that a Muranese glassworker, Pietro Bigaglia of Venice, displayed his "round shaped millefiori paperweights of transparent glass in which were inserted quantities of small tubes of all colors and forms assembled so as to look like a multitude of florets." Although some paperweights may have been produced in France prior to Bigaglia's display, it is generally accepted that this was the beginning of France's interest in producing paperweights as saleable objects.

During the classic period of millefiori and lampwork paperweight making (1840–1860), three outstanding glass factories in France set the pace in style and production of fine quality pieces: Compagnie des Cristalleries de Baccarat, Cristalleries de Saint Louis, and Clichy-la-Garenne. In a surprisingly short period of time, these French factories perfected the millefiori technique, introducing and developing the lampwork style as well. The high quality and the range of styles and design motifs created in France during this time have never been surpassed.

English glass factories were quick to imitate the French, and soon millefiori paperweights were being produced by factories in London and Birmingham. Prominent English makers in the nineteenth century were Bacchus, Whitefriars, and Islington.

In the United States, the production of paperweights in large numbers did not begin until after the New York Exhibition of the Industry of All Nations, held in New York City in 1853. Many of the early American weights were imitative of the French style: scrambled, close packed millefiori, and concentrics in clear glass or on latticinio grounds. However, the American makers were quick to contribute their own distinctive styles and techniques to paperweight making, particularly in the area of lampworking.

After about 1860 interest in paperweights tapered off in France, Britain and other European countries. It continued to flourish in America, with some production continuing intermittently into the early part of this century. The best-known American makers were the New England Glass Company, the Boston and Sandwich Glass Company, Gillinder, Mount Washington, and Millville.

Paperweight making was on the verge of becoming a lost art in the 1950s when Paul Jokelson, an importer and avid paperweight collector, approached the glass factories of Baccarat and Saint Louis with the idea of reviving the classic art. This was a difficult and challenging proposition, since paperweights had not been produced in significant numbers for more than eighty years. Artists and craftsmen spent nearly twenty years in research and experimentation rediscovering the techniques used in making sulphide, millefiori and lampwork paperweights. Once they succeeded, interest in contemporary paperweights blossomed.

Since that time several other glass factories, such as Perthshire in Scotland, have joined Baccarat and Saint Louis in producing fine quality modern paperweights. At the same time, individual glass artists are also producing paperweights. These contemporary factories and studio artists are responsible for the paperweight renaissance of the last thirty-five years. Their work has produced an exciting new generation of paperweights.

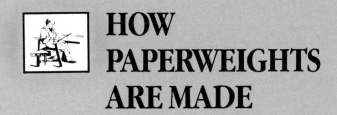

HOW PAPERWEIGHTS ARE MADE

HOW PAPERWEIGHTS
ARE MADE

The encasing process

Certain aspects of the paperweight making process, such as encasing a design in crystal, faceting, and finishing a piece, are the same for both millefiori and lampwork style weights. Once the millefiori canes or lampwork figures have been made they are arranged on a metal template and heated to just below the melting point. A metal collar is placed around the arrangement. The glassworker gathers a ball of molten glass on the end of a long iron pontil rod and rolls and works it into shape on a metal plate or "marver." He then lowers the red-hot glass into the collar and picks up the preheated design. This first gather of molten glass makes up the ground of the weight.

After the design is picked up, the piece is reheated in the "glory hole," the opening of the heating oven. Another gather of clear molten glass is added to form the dome of the weight. The worker rolls the pontil rod back and forth across the arms of his glassworking chair so that the still-soft glass will not sag or become misshapen. During this process the dome of the weight is shaped and smoothed with a wet wooden block or contoured pad of tissue or newspaper. While the glass is still pliable, tongs are used to form a slender neck at the base of the weight. When the piece has cooled sufficiently the worker gives a sharp tap to the pontil rod. The weight breaks off and falls into a bed of sand.

The next step is to gradually and evenly cool the weight in an annealing oven. This process is extremely critical. Sometimes the gathers of glass and design elements within a weight cool at different rates causing the piece to crack or shatter.

The final stage of the process is grinding and polishing. During this stage the "pontil mark" or scar that was made when the weight was separated from the pontil rod is ground down. Then, if desired, the dome of the weight is faceted or cut with a grinding wheel.

A paperweight is hand crafted during each step of its creation. Even if many weights of the same design are made by a glass factory, each has its own individual character.

Millefiori

The Italian word *millefiori* means "thousand flowers" and is used to describe the decorative elements which make up some of the most popular paperweight designs. The first step in making a millefiori paperweight is to produce a variety of glass rods or canes. The glassworker gathers molten glass from the furnace and works it into shape on a marver. If color is desired, the gather is rolled in colored glass powder, or colored glass is coated over the molten glass. It is then pressed into an iron mold and allowed to cool. Once the glass has hardened another gather of molten glass is added. The piece is again worked on the marver and pressed into a mold of a different shape. This process can be repeated several times to build layers of colors and designs within a rod.

At this stage the rod is about three inches in diameter and six inches long. The piece is reheated and another glassworker attaches a second pontil rod to the cane. The two workers quickly move apart, stretching the heated cane until it is pencil thin and sometimes over thirty feet long. The most uniformly stretched portions of the rod are

Picking up the bouquet

Shaping the dome

Attaching the second pontil rod

Stretching the cane

Complex millefiori canes

Lampworking

then cut into small pieces. Often several of these smaller rods are bundled together, heated, and stretched again to create a more complex cane. The design, no matter how intricate, is miniaturized. The cane is cut into tiny slices which are ground and polished for use within the paperweight.

Lampwork

Lampwork is a process of assembling and manipulating small components of colored glass into figures with the use of a hand torch. Thin glass rods of varying colors are heated with the torch and then formed into shape with small pliers, shears and other lampworking tools. Individual leaves, flower petals and stems are made in this way and then carefully assembled into a complete flower by reheating and attaching with the torch. These lampwork setups are arranged on a template, reheated, and encased in glass. Problems often occur when designs involve delicate and minute pieces, which can easily be distorted or cracked when touched by the first gather of molten glass.

Most studio artists produce lampwork paperweights. The major technical difference between paperweights made by studio artists and those produced in factories is the origin of the encasing glass. With few exceptions, studio artists work with commercially purchased solid glass slugs, melted down and shaped over a gas burner or "torch." The glass factories make their own glass by melting down raw materials in large furnaces, and gather the glass when encasing the design.

Sulphides

The creation of a sulphide is a complex and delicate process. The artist first prepares numerous drawings and detailed plans for the piece. A model five times the size of the cameo is then made from plastic modeling clay. Special attention must be paid to the details of the sculpture to allow for the eventual five-to-one reduction of the design. The model is cast in plaster, the surface is refined, and minute changes are made. From this piece the caster makes a bronze portrait which is polished and mounted on a reduction plate where a faithful reproduction, one-fifth the size of the bronze image, is cut into steel.

A carefully prepared mixture of clay, sand and soapstone is poured into a plaster cast made from the steel mold. The cameo is hydraulically pressed and heat treated, placed on a circular steel plate, and then gently covered with a gather of molten crystal. Another mass of clear or colored glass is added to form the ground of the weight. Then the piece is annealed, polished, and faceted if desired.

ANTIQUE PAPERWEIGHTS

ANTIQUE AMERICAN

PAPERWEIGHT MAKING arrived in the United States in the 1850s almost a decade after its appearance in Europe. It is believed that American glass factories first became interested in paperweight production after viewing the European weights on display at the Great Exhibition in London in 1851. It is likely, however, that Americans traveling abroad in the 1840s had also seen examples of paperweight making.

Many early American weights were imitative of the French-style scrambled, close millefiori, and concentric patterns set on clear glass or on latticinio grounds. In general, the American weights contained canes which were less complex in structure than the French. However, the American makers quickly infused their own style into their work and branched off into a variety of creative lampwork subjects.

Three American glass factories stand out as principal paperweight producers in these early years: the New England Glass Company of East Cambridge, Massachusetts (NEGC); the Boston and Sandwich Glass Company at Sandwich on Cape Cod, Massachusetts; and the Mount Washington Glass Works of South Boston and New Bedford, Massachusetts. All three factories were founded by Deming Jarves, an enterprising Boston merchant. The three factories often drew from the same group of skilled craftsmen, many of whom came from European apprenticeships. Occasionally, these craftsmen swapped millefiori rods. It is therefore often difficult to distinguish between the paperweights made at each factory, though each glasshouse had a distinct history and reputation.

Another American factory which was well known for its paperweights is Whitall Tatum and Company, in Millville, New Jersey. As early as the 1860s, workers at Millville were experimenting with paperweight making during their off hours. Over the years a variety of distinctly American styles and design motifs were developed at Millville including the factory's most famous design, the Millville rose.

Paperweight making was practiced longer in the United States than in Europe, with some production continuing intermittently into the early part of the twentieth century.

1 Concentric rings of pastel millefiori canes set over a clear ground surround a bold geometric cane. $325

2 Two ripe red apples on a stem with four serrated leaves are set over a clear ground. $650

3 Arranged on a stem with four leaves, two brightly striped apples are set over a clear ground. $950

4 In this symmetrically arranged fruit weight, five golden pears and four red cherries are clustered on a white latticinio cushion. $850

5 Set on a ground of white latticinio, this upright bouquet is made up of an arrangement of lampwork and millefiori flowers with several deep green serrated leaves. $2450

6 In this unusual weight, a yellow lampwork vase with an open-weave latticinio ground is filled with a bouquet of lush red roses. $1600

7 Eight colorful spokes of pastel complex millefiori canes radiate from a brightly colored complex cane set on a bed of latticinio. $450

8 A blue and white jasper ground provides a striking contrast for a well-formed red poinsettia with two green leaves and millefiori stamens. $850

9 This crown weight contains white filigree twists between red, white, and green ribbon twists with a complex millefiori cane in the center. $500

10 A deep blue double clematis with three leaves and a graceful tendril is set over a white latticinio ground. $1200

11 A handsome red poinsettia with millefiori cane stamens and three green leaves is encased in clear glass. $600

12 In this unusual leaf bouquet three green and two peach and yellow shaded leaves are presented on a well-formed latticinio cushion. $1400

13 Eight brilliant flowers encircle the lampwork inscription "M . E KEENE 1914" on a clear ground. $375

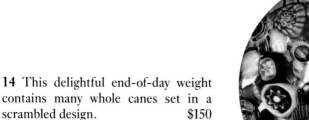

14 This delightful end-of-day weight contains many whole canes set in a scrambled design. $150

15 This exceedingly rare magnum weight contains a Mount Washington rose with two buds encircled by a garland of small blue flowers set over a clear ground. $20,000

16 A richly colored Millville rose with dark green leaves is enclosed in this handsome pedestal weight. $1500

17 A bold American eagle is the subject of this pedestal frit weight; the design was created with glass dust. $1850

18 In this design a three-dimensional apple, ripening from yellow to peach, is set on a cookie base. $1400

ANTIQUE BACCARAT

THE GLASS FACTORY that is today called Compagnie des Cristalleries de Baccarat was founded in 1764 under the name Verrerie de Sainte Anne. Located in the Alsace-Lorraine region of France within fifty miles of Cristalleries de Saint Louis, Verrerie de Sainte Anne specialized in plate glass, mirrors, and a wide range of utilitarian glassware. During the 1820s the factory, which had by then started producing fine lead glass, was sold and renamed Cristalleries de Baccarat.

In 1846, under the management of Emile Godard, the craftsmen at Baccarat perfected the production of millefiori paperweights. By 1848 exquisite lampwork flowers, bouquets, butterflies and other motifs were also being produced. Paperweight manufacture at Baccarat was a small but significant part of the company's production for almost twenty years.

Baccarat excelled in the making of silhouette canes, which were frequently used in carpet grounds, trefoils, mushrooms, overlays and close packed weights. Eighteen of the best-known Baccarat silhouettes, called the Gridel series, were based on the paper cutout designs created in 1847 by Joseph Emile Gridel, the nine-year-old nephew of Jean-Baptiste Toussaint, Baccarat's manager at the time.

Less than a quarter of the antique paperweights produced by Baccarat contain date or signature canes. When a signature cane is present it is always accompanied by a date cane; some date canes appear alone. Date canes are comprised of four distinct rods fused together, with a single numeral in each rod.

19 A red and white primrose with a double ring of stardust cane stamens is set over a stem with six leaves set over a clear ground. $1200

20 Three stems with leaves surround this attractive six-petal red and white primrose with stardust cane stamens over a clear base. $1100

21 A primrose with five red petals edged in white is enhanced by several unusually shaped green leaves on a clear ground. $900

22 A honeycomb cane makes up the center of this attractive five-petaled red and white primrose with one red bud set over a clear ground. $1750

23 A yellow primrose with orange decoration on each petal and a single bud are set in clear glass with a star-cut base. A complex stardust cane forms the center of the flower. $2950

24 A border of alternating red and white millefiori canes surrounds this lampwork primrose with one red bud and honeycomb cane stamens. $2250

25 Set on an upset muslin ground and encircled by canes of alternating colors, this magnificent weight presents a double clematis with veined red petals, one bud, and stardust stamens. $3850

26 A deep red double clematis with honeycomb cane stamens and a bud is set on a lace ground and surrounded by green and white millefiori canes. $3600

27 A purple double clematis with veined petals and stardust cane stamens with a stem, green leaves and a bud is set over a clear crystal ground. $1850

28 This miniature weight contains a blue and white wallflower with honeycomb cane stamens, three leaves and a tiny red bud. The blossom is encircled by a ring of alternating red and white millefiori canes and set over a clear star-cut base. $1750

29 Set over a clear star-cut base, this purple and white wallflower has a complex arrowhead cane center. The flower is surrounded by a millefiori border with more arrowhead canes. $3500

30 This blue and white six-petaled primrose with five sets of leaves is set over a clear ground and bordered by a ring of alternating purple and white millefiori canes. $2200

31 A handsome white anemone with blue edging and cupped flower petals is enhanced by stardust cane stamens and deep green elongated leaves. The design is set over a clear star-cut base. $1100

32 Set over a clear star-cut base, this attractive blue and white primrose with a large honeycomb cane center is set off by five light green serrated leaves and a small blue bud. $1100

33 A colorful millefiori-winged butter-fly with a dark amethyst latticinio body hovers over a white double clematis and bud set over a clear star-cut base. $3950

34 Alternating red and white millefiori canes surround a white double clematis with deeply veined petals and a complex arrowhead cane center set over a clear star-cut base. $2350

35 A delicate white wheatflower with blue dots on the petals, a complex cane center, and serrated leaves is set over a clear star-cut base. $2200

36 This faceted weight has a double white clematis with deeply veined petals and a complex cane center. The flower is surrounded by green leaves and set over a clear star-cut ground. $2800

37 A pompon with numerous close-set blue and white petals and a bright red bud is encircled by a border of alternating green and white canes, all over a clear star-cut base. $4500

38 A salmon-colored pompon with two buds is set over a clear star-cut base with a border of alternating blue arrowhead and white stardust canes. $3200

39 Six pink clematis buds are symmetrically arranged on a green stem with leaves. The design is enhanced by faceting and a clear star-cut base. $1950

40 A traditional Baccarat pansy with deep purple and yellow petals, a honey-comb cane center, and a single bud is encircled by a distinctive millefiori border of alternating green and white canes. $2400

41 A Baccarat pansy with a single bud and stardust cane stamens is set over a clear ground. $750

42 This extraordinary bouquet is made up of two unusual pansies with lower petals of blue and white millefiori arrow-head canes, one double white clematis with deeply veined petals, a thousand-petal rose bud, and a single red bud. The weight is faceted and set over a clear star-cut base. $11,000

43 Covered with an arrangement of colorful flowers, this extremely rare white overlay painted weight has side facets and a clear star-cut base. $2200

44 A graceful butterfly with millefiori wings and an amethyst latticinio body is set over a clear star-cut base and ringed by a millefiori border of alternating green and white canes. $2950

45 This attractive end-of-day weight made up of many pieces of white latticinio has a lacy, light appearance typical of Baccarat scrambled millefiori weights. $375

46 With blue and white arrowhead canes at its center, a garland of white stardust canes intertwines with a garland of eight-pointed red and white canes in this magnificent design. The weight is encased by a green flash overlay, faceted, and set over a clear star-cut base. $4300

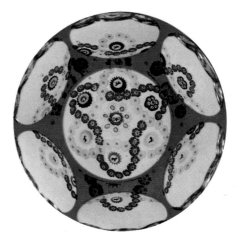

47 Encased in a wine-colored flash overlay, this beautiful garland weight includes seven Gridel animal silhouettes —a dog, a squirrel, a deer, a rooster, a goat and two butterflies. $4800

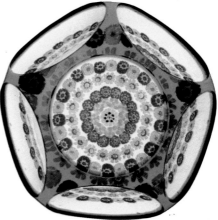

48 Rings of millefiori canes including green shamrocks, white stardust canes and alternating red and white canes make up this brilliant concentric motif encased by a green flash overlay. $3200

49 Made up of unmelted bits of silica, sand and mica, rock weights such as this one are thought to have been given away as souvenirs by the Baccarat factory around 1848. $275

50 This finely crafted cameo of Napoleon is set over a ruby flash ground with diamond-cut sides. $900

51 An exceptionally fine sulphide depicting a hunter and dog in the woods is set over a translucent ruby ground with diamond-cut sides. $3200

52 This colorful close packed millefiori includes a blue and white Gridel silhouette cane of a squirrel and a B1847 date/signature cane. $1000

53 Several Gridel silhouette canes (dog, butterfly, goat, deer, and bird) are included in this rich blue and white millefiori carpet ground weight. It is signed and dated B1848 in white canes with colored numerals. $5500

54 Large complex millefiori on a ground of upset muslin surround a center cane which includes several honeycomb canes with turquoise centers. $4200

55 This scattered millefiori design includes many bold Gridel silhouette canes including a butterfly, horse, deer, dog, elephant, hunter, and rooster. Set on a bed of upset muslin which includes colored ribbon twists in some of the latticinio sections, the weight is signed and dated B1848 with red, blue and green numerals in a white field. $1800

56 A charming miniature spaced millefiori on lace with a large red, white and blue arrowhead cane contains three Gridel silhouette canes: a goat, dog, and horse. $800

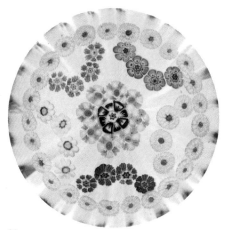

57 An outer ring of stardust canes with green bull's-eye centers encircles a delicate star pattern millefiori motif. Set over a clear deep star-cut base, the central complex cane includes eight arrowheads in alternating colors. $650

58 On a clear ground, four loops of red and white millefiori radiate from a circle of complex blue canes which surrounds a center made up of arrowheads of alternating colors. $650

59 This interesting patterned millefiori weight was made some time after the classic period. Paperweights of this type are known as Dupont weights, named for the craftsman supposed to have made them after 1870. $150

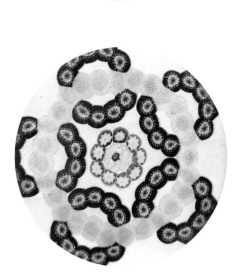

60 The middle ring of canes within this appealing miniature millefiori weight is made up of stardust canes with blue and white bull's-eye centers. The large central cane has green arrowhead canes tucked into alternate corners of the six-pointed star. $450

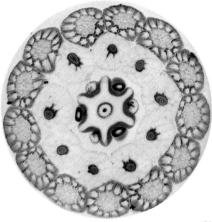

61 In this classic Baccarat mushroom, a blue and white torsade encircles a close packed millefiori tuft over a clear star-cut base. $1600

62 In this unusual design, an outer circle of pulled stardust canes forms a white stem for this close packed millefiori mushroom surrounded by a blue and white spiraling torsade. $2100

63 An enormous variety of complex canes, including Gridel animal silhouettes of a goat, deer, horse, hunter, and dog, makes up this brilliant close packed millefiori design. The weight is signed and dated B1848 in a cane with red, green and blue on a white field. $1650

CLICHY

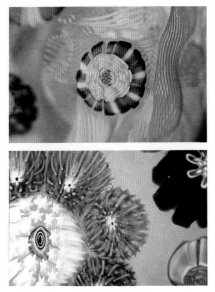

Because of the destruction of company records, very little is known about Clichy-la-Garenne, the last to be established of the three great paperweight producing glass factories in France. Founded by Messrs. Rouyer and Maes in about 1838, the factory first produced inexpensive glass for export. But by the 1840s, both Saint Louis and Baccarat were concerned about Clichy's rapid growth and the improved quality of their glassware.

As early as 1844, Clichy exhibited with Baccarat and Saint Louis in Paris, where the young company's colored glass and overlaid glass were highly praised. Clichy also created quite a stir when they developed a new type of glass which was much lighter than the traditional lead glass yet retained the desirable optical properties of conventional crystal.

It is thought that Clichy may have started producing paperweights as part of a stratagem to entice customers away from the more established glass factories. In a letter to Saint Louis, a Paris retail firm wrote:

"The selling of weights has now gone mostly to Clichy which cannot fulfill all the orders received. This article (paperweights) has given a great importance to this factory by the contracts that were established through it with buyers who were not in the habit of applying there."

Clichy produced some of the most magnificent weights of the classic period. Their colors were brilliant and many of their cane and weight designs were unique and distinctive. The Clichy rose, considered a trademark of the factory, frequently appears in their pieces. Clichy is also well known for its lush moss carpet ground weights.

Very few Clichy weights are signed or dated. The most frequently used signature cane is a "C" in either serif or sans-serif style. An extremely rare signature is a cane which contains the factory name in full. Clichy also used the "C" scroll garland motif as a signature in some weights.

64 This magnificent and extremely rare pedestal weight with alternating green and white stave sides includes five pink and green Clichy roses around a central pastry mold cane. A ring of eighteen green and white roses and a circle with several white roses edged in green are also part of the design. $27, 000

65 A rare and spectacular Clichy bouquet is made up of a lampwork pansy and three millefiori flowers: a pink and green rose, and two purple thistles. The bouquet, tied at the base with a pink ribbon, is set over a clear ground. $14,500

66 A very unusual white lampwork flower with stardust cane stamens is set on a lush carpet ground of prairie moss canes. $11,500

67 Rings of complex canes, edelweiss canes and moss-edged canes encircle a pink and green Clichy rose set against a rich royal blue ground. $1500

68 Concentric rings of vividly colored Clichy canes are set over a tomato-red ground in this jewel-like miniature weight. $800

69 An interesting array of classic Clichy canes, including a perfectly formed pink and green rose and a superb white and green rose, is arranged in a spaced millefiori design against a midnight blue ground. $2600

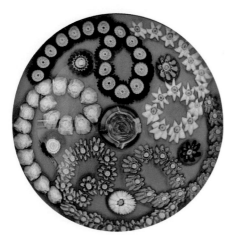

70 Set against a striking turquoise ground, five loops of millefiori canes, one made up entirely of white and green roses and another made up of brilliant white edelweiss canes, are arranged around a large pink and green Clichy rose. $3600

71 A graceful millefiori trefoil design made up of complex red and white canes is enhanced by seven large pastry mold canes and set against a deep turquoise ground. $2650

72 A circle of stardust canes and a ring of complex millefiori are concentrically arranged around a large pink and green Clichy rose set over a brilliant turquoise ground. $1500

73 This classic cobalt blue and white Clichy swirl has a large yellow, white and red complex millefiori cane at the center of the design. $1250

74 A pink and white swirl radiates from a cobalt blue, white, and pink complex central cane. $1350

75 In this miniature a deep blue and white swirl emanates from a green and white cane center. $950

76 A rare blue-over-white double over-lay encases a concentric millefiori mushroom made up of subtle shades of pink, white and green. The base, which is clear and star-cut, reflects in the side facets. $7500

77 In this concentric millefiori sur-rounded by a pink and white stave bas-ket, one ring is made up of ten well-formed pink and green roses alternating with edelweiss canes. The star-cut base is reflected in the side facets. $6000

78 This festive Clichy barber-pole che-quer has several complex canes and a magnificent green-edged white rose in the center. $1750

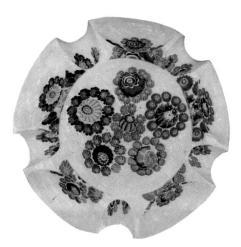

79 Six brightly colored circles of mille-fiori, each surrounding a large pastry mold cane, make up this patterned millefiori design on upset muslin. The weight is enhanced by faceting. $1750

80 A distinctive complex cane is set in each of the five loops of this brightly colored cinquefoil arrangement. A well-formed pink and green Clichy rose is at the center. $2500

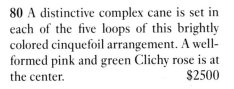

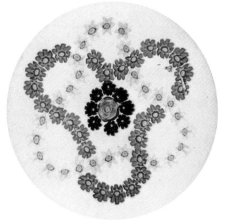

81 Two intertwining trefoil loops, one made up entirely of edelweiss canes, frame a perfect pink and green Clichy rose encircled by a ring of purple mille-fiori. $1800

82 Fashioned in complementary shades of pink and green, this five-flower mille-fiori nosegay with well-formed lamp-work leaves is surrounded by a ring of millefiori canes. Set in faceted clear glass over a star-cut base. $1250

83 In this miniature weight, a three-flower millefiori nosegay with five deeply serrated lampwork leaves is set over a clear ground. $650

84 Five loops of alternating pink and blue millefiori canes with a green and white center cane make up this beauti-fully faceted weight. $1200

85 Eight bold and colorful pastry mold canes surround a pink, white and green center cane in this miniature spaced millefiori weight. $500

86 This delightful design, set over a clear ground, has a variety of fine Clichy canes, including a central green and pink rose and a white rose with stripes of pale pink. $850

87 In this miniature concentric millefiori weight, a full white Clichy rose is encircled by ten deep green canes and an outer ring of pastry mold canes. $600

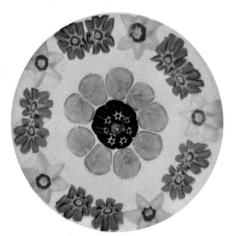

88 A striking purple, white and green cane is surrounded by a ring of nine perfectly formed pink and green Clichy roses and a border of green canes alternating with edelweiss canes. This miniature concentric weight is set in clear glass. $600

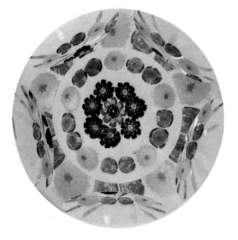

89 A pattern of two pink and green roses alternating with one white stardust cane makes up the outer ring in this delightful concentric millefiori weight. A clear star-cut base reflects in each of the side facets. $700

90 A magnificent white and purple Clichy rose is at the center of this beautifully designed concentric millefiori over a clear ground. $800

42

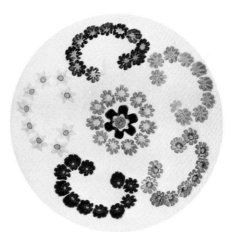

91 Five open loops of millefiori placed around a large green cane and a ring of delicate pink canes make up this distinctive Clichy "C" scroll design. $1250

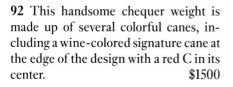

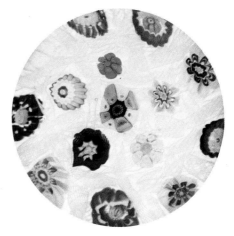

92 This handsome chequer weight is made up of several colorful canes, including a wine-colored signature cane at the edge of the design with a red C in its center. $1500

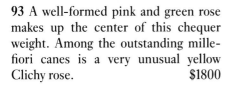

93 A well-formed pink and green rose makes up the center of this chequer weight. Among the outstanding millefiori canes is a very unusual yellow Clichy rose. $1800

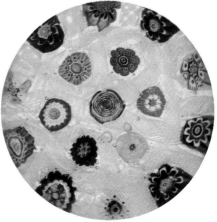

94 A very rare purple and yellow pansy with a bud and green leaves is set over a clear ground. $1700

95 An exquisite pink and green rose is at the center of this striking turquoise and white Clichy swirl. $3500

96 This delightful end-of-day millefiori weight includes several small pieces of Clichy roses and one large section of a pink and white rose cane. $350

ANTIQUE SAINT LOUIS

THE HISTORY OF Cristalleries de Saint Louis, one of the major paperweight producing factories of the classic period (1840–1860), dates back to 1767. Originally named Verrerie Royale de Saint Louis for King Saint Louis of France, the factory was established in the Munzthal Forest in the Lorraine region of France, an ideal location because of the abundance of wood, sand and potash.

Throughout the early eighteenth century, France had lagged behind other countries in Europe in the production of fine glass. But by 1772, Saint Louis was producing lead glass equal in quality to the highly valued flint glass of England. In 1782 the factory was the first in France to perfect the manufacture of crystal. Because of the fierce competition in the glass industry, revealing trade secrets was decreed a crime punishable by death. Workers had to obtain permission to travel more than one mile from the factory, and two years' notice was required in order to resign from the Saint Louis staff.

It is not surprising that Saint Louis, which was in the forefront of fine glass production, was the first of the glass factories in France to begin producing paperweights. One of their earliest millefiori weights is dated 1845, and by 1848 the factory was producing a wide range of lampwork pieces as well.

Saint Louis displayed paperweights in many of the Paris exhibitions. The last recorded showing of Saint Louis weights was at the Paris Exposition in 1867. Interest in the objects was on the decline and a creative and rich era of paperweight making was drawing to a close.

Few antique Saint Louis paperweights are signed or dated. When present, Saint Louis date canes are constructed with the numerals appearing in separate rods fused together with the "SL" cane appearing above the date. The numerals of date canes are done in single colors; either red, blue or black. Date canes are always accompanied by a signature cane; however, there are instances of signature canes appearing alone.

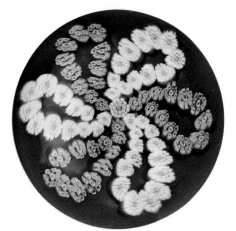

97 A graceful pinwheel design made up of loops of white stardust canes alternating with loops of pink and white canes is set over a deep turquoise ground. $3200

98 An elegant upright bouquet of lampwork and millefiori flowers is encircled by a blue and white torsade. The star-cut base is clear and the sides are allover faceted. $3200

99 Brightly colored bits of millefiori and several whole canes make up this vivid scrambled millefiori design. $375

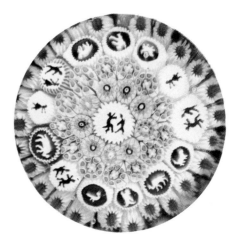

100 An unusually large number of silhouette canes, including four pairs of dancing devils, a dog with a monkey on its back, three camels, and several others, makes up this exceptional close concentric weight. $6500

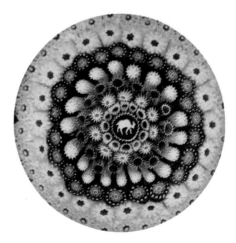

101 A well-defined blue and white camel silhouette cane forms the center of this close packed concentric millefiori weight. $3200

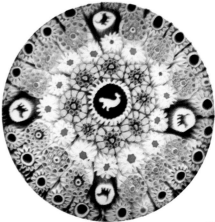

102 Four dog silhouette canes combine with close concentric circles of millefiori in this handsome weight with a duck silhouette cane center. $3750

103 Shades of blue, green, salmon and white make up this close packed concentric millefiori design. $2650

104 This close packed millefiori weight has five concentric rings of typical Saint Louis canes around a central complex cane. $2100

105 Magnificent sky-blue and white canes predominate in this very unusual close packed concentric millefiori weight with a large red, white and green complex cane center. $3400

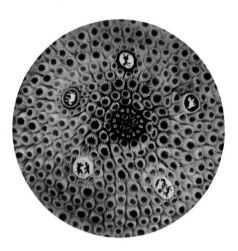

106 This pink carpet ground weight containing five silhouettes and a central complex cane is edged by pale green hollow canes. $4900

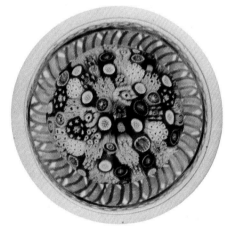

107 Pink, pistachio, red and blue canes are arranged in this close packed millefiori mushroom weight encircled by a salmon and white torsade. $3800

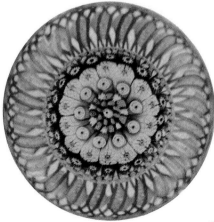

108 A salmon-colored torsade surrounds a close packed concentric millefiori mushroom design in complementary shades of pink, pistachio, blue and white. $3800

109 This close packed millefiori mushroom, resembling a Baccarat design, is surrounded by a distinctive Saint Louis torsade: a white latticinio twist wrapped with a blue ribbon. $2500

110 Vividly colored millefiori canes are arranged in a striking close concentric mushroom pattern surrounded by a blue and white torsade. $2900

111 Alternating segments of red and blue jasper ground are divided by white rods with a ring of millefiori surrounding a center cane. $300

112 Multiple images of two deep red cherries hanging on a branch with green leaves are seen through the many small facets on this weight. $2500

113 A full, deeply veined purple dahlia with five barely visible green leaves is set over a clear ground in this spectacular weight. $3850

114 A richly colored complex cane forms the center of this pink dahlia surrounded by six green leaves. $1600

115 A delicate white pompon with one bud and four dark green leaves is set in clear crystal with side faceting. The unfaceted top portion of the weight magnifies the diamond-cut base. $1650

116 A pink dahlia with veined petals, a large millefiori center, and four leaves is set over a clear ground. $1900

117 This perfectly formed white camomile and bud with four leaves is set over a dazzling pink latticinio ground. $2600

118 A dark blue double clematis with millefiori stamens is enhanced by a latticinio ground and side facets. $1500

119 This deep pink double clematis with matchhead cane stamens and five leaves is set on white latticinio. $1200

120 This realistic fuchsia includes buds and dark green leaves on a ground of white latticinio. $2950

121 A four-flower millefiori nosegay bordered by a ring of multicolored canes is set on an upset muslin ground. $950

122 An amber flash ground sets off this millefiori nosegay with deeply serrated leaves. The design is enhanced by seven small facets around a single top facet and six large side facets. $800

123 A ring of complex canes surrounds a well-formed millefiori nosegay with five leaves set over an amber flash diamond-cut ground. $1100

124 A beautifully formed snow-white pompon with bud and deep green leaves is circled by a ring of pistachio and white canes alternating with blue and white millefiori canes. The design is set over a clear ground and has one top facet and six side facets. $3200

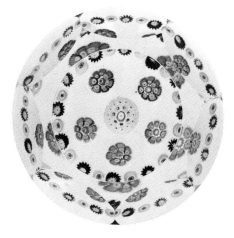

125 In this miniature weight a patterned millefiori design is set over a clear ground with one top facet and seven side facets. $400

126 Red, white and blue are the predominant cane colors in this handsome close packed concentric millefiori mushroom surrounded by a blue and white torsade. The weight is cut with one top facet and six deep side facets. $2700

127 This superb crown weight has radiating twisted ribbons in red and green and pistachio and blue divided by delicate latticinio twists. $2800

128 Red and green twisted ribbons alternate with lacy twists of latticinio in this beautifully designed crown weight with a white stardust cane center. $3800

129 Two luscious ripe pears, a peach, and three brilliant red cherries are set on a bed of green leaves over a white latticinio ground. $1600

130 In this elegantly simple design a well-formed four-flower millefiori nosegay with realistic green leaves is encased in clear glass and faceted. $950

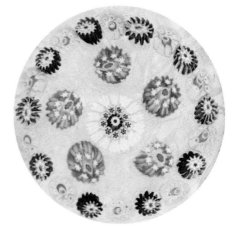

131 A bright, sunny patterned millefiori design arranged around a white stardust complex cane is set over a lacy ground of upset muslin in this miniature. $600

132 A well-formed upright bouquet made up of a large yellow lampwork flower surrounded by three lampwork and three millefiori flowers is enhanced by a top facet and six side facets. $2450

OTHER ANTIQUES

THIS SECTION INCLUDES paperweights produced during the classic period by Bohemian glass factories and by Bacchus, Whitefriars, and Val St. Lambert. It also includes Pinchbeck weights.

Although not much is known about Bohemian weights, it is believed that most of these pieces were made between 1846 and 1849. A majority of the Bohemian weights are scattered millefiori on lace and often include silhouette canes which can help in identification. A number of overlays were also produced.

The glassworks of Bacchus and Sons was located in Birmingham, a main center of glassmaking activity in England during the 1800s. "Letter weights," as they were sometimes called, were never more than a small part of the company's production; however, they did attract attention. Most of the pieces made by Bacchus are large in size—over three inches in diameter—and all contain millefiori.

Whitefriars, the English glass factory named for the Carmelite monks whose monastery was once located on the factory site, began making paperweights around 1848. Antique Whitefriars weights are characterized by the use of concentric millefiori spacing schemes.

The Belgian glass factory of Val St. Lambert produced mostly patterned millefiori paperweights. Although weights from this factory are rare, Val St. Lambert is also known to have made lampwork pieces, sulphides, and some overlays.

Pinchbeck weights derive their name from the seventeenth-century clockmaker Christopher Pinchbeck, who developed a copper-zinc alloy closely resembling gold. The word Pinchbeck became a synonym for counterfeit or cheap. Pinchbeck weights, which have become highly collectible in recent years, are made up of a bas-relief metal insert held by a base of copper, tin, or some other substance, covered (rather than encased) by a glass dome.

133 This distinctive Pinchbeck weight honors the British general and statesman Arthur Wellesley, first Duke of Wellington (1769–1852). The name "Wellington" appears in relief at the right of the bust. $1100

134 This Pinchbeck squirrel eating a nut is cast in a silver color instead of the usual gold. $950

135 A forest scene with a hunter and two dogs is the subject of this well-detailed Pinchbeck weight. $1000

136 A bold concentric millefiori design in shades of blue, turquoise, pink and white makes up this attractive Whitefriars weight. $200

137 In this weight by Whitefriars, vivid red, white and blue canes with cruciform centers are arranged in a concentric millefiori pattern. $150

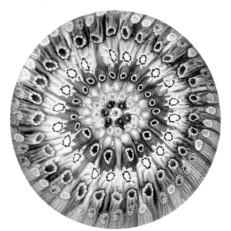

138 This Whitefriars concentric millefiori design includes two rings of hollow canes. $250

139 Deep blue and white spokes form the background for this Bohemian patterned millefiori weight. A tiny silhouette of a monkey is at the center of one of the white millefiori canes. $750

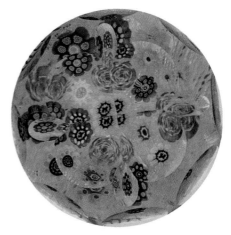

140 This delicately colored Bohemian spaced millefiori on lace includes animal silhouettes and four Clichy-type roses. It is cut with a quatrefoil facet on the top and eight side facets. $1100

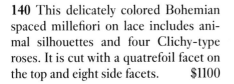

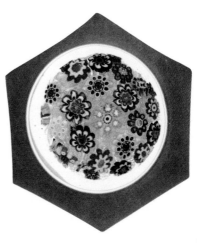

141 A red-over-white double overlay frames this attractive Bohemian scattered millefiori on lace design. A tiny silhouette of a hunter and dog can be found near the edge. $2100

142 Included in this Bohemian scattered millefiori on upset muslin are an eagle silhouette cane and a double silhouette cane of a hunter and dog. $400

143 In this Val St. Lambert weight a ruby flash overlay is cut with a star design on top and flowers and vines on the side to reveal a clear interior. $350

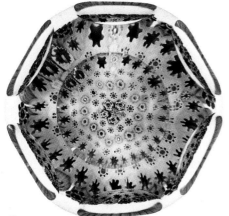

144 Characteristic pastel shades accented by deep red make up this beautifully designed close concentric millefiori weight by Bacchus. $1100

CONTEMPORARY
PAPERWEIGHTS

RICK AYOTTE

RICK AYOTTE is the only contemporary glass artist specializing in lampwork bird paperweights. A paperweight artist since 1976, Ayotte's colorful and finely detailed birds are often set in naturalistic surroundings which include intricate foliage, blossoms, berries, butterflies, and nests.

A native of Nashua, New Hampshire, Ayotte studied at Lowell Technological Institute and later took a job as a scientific glassblower. In 1970 he started his own business, Ayotte's Artistry in Glass, which specialized in novelty glassware and gifts. While working in the scientific glassblowing industry, Ayotte became acquainted with glass artist Paul Stankard, who first introduced him to the idea of making paperweights. Ayotte found paperweight making a creative challenge as well as an opportunity to combine his skill and expertise in glass with a longtime interest in ornithology.

Ayotte's fascination with birds began when he was in high school. During that time he charted migratory bird groups and studied their food and eating habits. He also began carving life-size birds from wood.

Ayotte's glass paperweights reflect his knowledge and love of ornithology as well as his mastery of the art of glassmaking. His colors are vibrant and alive, and his birds and environments are accurate and realistic. He has also developed a compound layering technique, which involves creating two separate encased layers within a weight. This technique has given him the ability to achieve unusual depth and dimension in his work.

Ayotte produces paperweights in editions of twenty-five to seventy-five pieces, and signs his work with an engraved "Ayotte" on the base.

145 A golden-fronted leafbird is perched in a tropical golden shower tree with blossoms and seed pods in this colorful compound weight. $550

146 An orange and yellow flowering quince surrounds a finely crafted winter wren set over a clear ground. $475

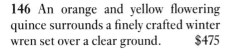

147 A male and female screech owl resting on a pine branch with cones and delicate green needles are set over a clear ground. $450

148 In this spring garden scene, a cottontail rabbit and a brightly colored butterfly are surrounded by a variety of flowers. $450

149 A red-breasted bluebird sits on a branch of pale pink trailing arbutus over a clear ground. $450

150 In this weight Ayotte has captured the nearly invisible image of the ruby-throated hummingbird's wings in motion as it hovers over a bough of bright orange trumpetflowers. $450

151 A dark blue *Pyrrhopyge creon* butterfly with black edging on its wings hovers over a branch with pale yellow blossoms. Set over a clear ground. $475

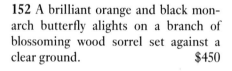

152 A brilliant orange and black monarch butterfly alights on a branch of blossoming wood sorrel set against a clear ground. $450

153 A scarlet tanager sits in a bright yellow blossom-filled tulip tree set over a clear ground. $550

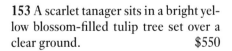

154 In this compound weight with two separately encased layers, a handsome red-breasted robin rests in a flowering dogwood tree. $550

155 A lively blue jay perches in a flowering wild rhododendron in this compound design set against a clear ground. $550

156 In this whimsical weight a mouse atop a toadstool gazes at a colorful crocus garden and a butterfly. $600

MODERN BACCARAT

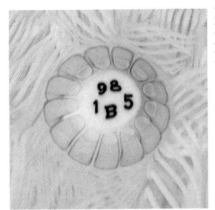

DURING THE 1950s, Compagnie des Cristalleries de Baccarat, one of the three major paperweight-producing glass factories of the classic period (1840–1860), became involved in reviving the art of paperweight making. Interest in paperweights began to grow in 1951 when a magnificent antique millefiori weight was found in the ruins of an old church at Baccarat. Then in 1953 paperweight collector and connoisseur Paul Jokelson suggested that Baccarat experiment with sulphide making. That year the factory produced its first successful contemporary sulphide commemorating the coronation of Queen Elizabeth II of England. This paperweight, which portrays the Queen and the Duke of Edinburgh in double profile, was one of the first cameo incrustations to be produced by a glass factory in almost 100 years.

By 1957, after several years of research and experimentation, Baccarat had also perfected the millefiori paperweight making process and began producing quality millefiori weights in limited editions. In 1970 Baccarat revived the Gridel silhouette canes which had been considered a trademark of the factory's millefiori work during the nineteenth century. In the contemporary series a large central Gridel silhouette cane is surrounded by smaller Gridel silhouettes and various arrangements of other millefiori canes.

In addition to sulphides and millefiori designs, Baccarat also produces paperweights which feature imaginative and finely crafted lampwork motifs. While several of the contemporary flower and lampwork arrangements are based on classic lampwork weights, Baccarat's glass craftsmen have also developed many distinctive new designs.

Contemporary Baccarat weights are signed with an acid-etched seal of the company which includes the words "Baccarat, France," and the outlined forms of a goblet, decanter and tumbler. An interior date/signature cane and the number of the item are often included in special limited edition weights. Most Baccarat sulphides are inscribed on the edge of the bust with one or more of the following: the artist's name, the year the sculpture was created, and the name of the subject.

157 Set against a deep blue ground, a yellow ladybug rests on the leaf of a crocus flower with orange stamens and bud. The weight is signed B1983 in a cane at the base of the stem. $400

158 A graceful stem of red and white dicentra is set over a white latticinio ground. Signed B1984 in a cane. $450

159 The largest sulphide ever made, this dramatic weight contains a cameo of Mount Rushmore enhanced by a red-over-white double overlay with one large oval top facet and eight smaller side facets. $400

160 This cameo of Martin Luther by sulphide artist Gilbert Poillerat is set over a blue flash grid-cut base. $325

161 Fashioned by Gilbert Poillerat, this classic portrait of George Washington is set in faceted crystal against a translucent green ground. $325

162 Created in 1953 to commemorate the coronation of Queen Elizabeth II, this sulphide of the Queen and H. R. H. the Duke of Edinburgh was one of the first modern sulphides produced by Baccarat. The cameo, sculpted by Gilbert Poillerat, is framed by a red-over-white double overlay on a clear grid-cut base. $450

163 A silhouette cane of a dog is surrounded by patterned millefiori, including an outer ring of seventeen smaller Gridel silhouette canes. $300

164 This finely sculpted sulphide of President John F. Kennedy is highlighted by dramatic diamond-cut faceting. $500

165 First in the series produced by Gilbert Poillerat commemorating American presidents, this sulphide of President Eisenhower is faceted and set over a clear fan-cut base. $400

166 Seventeen miniature Gridel silhouette canes divide a circle pattern of millefiori surrounding a large stork cane set against a royal blue ground. $300

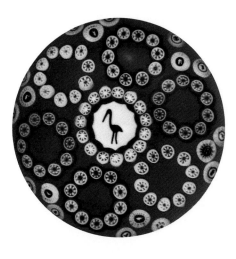

167 All eighteen Gridel animal silhouette canes can be found in this weight; a large silhouette of a goat is at the center. Set on a dark butterscotch ground. $300

168 Alternating panels of green and blue millefiori divided by Gridel silhouettes surround a large Gridel monkey in the center. $300

RAY AND BOB BANFORD

RAY AND BOB BANFORD, father and son, began their paperweight making careers in 1971. Working together in a studio in back of their family home in Hammonton, New Jersey, the two artists share ideas and techniques while remaining independent craftsmen with distinct and individual styles.

Ray first became intrigued by the idea of making paperweights after watching an elderly Czechoslovakian glass craftsman in Vineland, New Jersey. A visit to the Corning Museum also served as inspiration, and in 1971 Ray began to try his hand at the process.

Bob worked as a scientific glassblower for a year and a half after graduating from high school. He then began demonstrating novelty glass work and in his spare time experimented with paperweights. In 1971, along with his father, Bob seriously began to produce weights.

Ray's paperweights include bouquets of lampwork roses, irises, lilies-of-the-valley, and morning glories, as well as several other types of flowers. He is especially well-known for his extraordinary rose paperweights.

Bob's work, like his father's, has been greatly influenced by classic style French paperweights. He includes single flowers, intricate upright and flat bouquets, dragonflies, bumblebees, salamanders and snakes in his designs. Bob's finely crafted lampwork weights are in a number of private and public collections including the Smithsonian Institution, the Corning Museum of Glass, the Chicago Art Institute, and the Bergstrom-Mahler Museum.

The Banfords are among the few studio artists who produce overlay paperweights. They are also known for their elaborate basket and gingham cutting designs.

Each of Bob's weights contains a signature cane made up of a red "B" in a white ground surrounded by a blue rim. Most of Ray's work is signed in a cane with a black "B" on a white ground; however, some of his early pieces contain signature canes in a variety of color combinations.

169 Deep green leaves set in a cross-shaped arrangement and a well-formed white lampwork flower with yellow upright stamens are set over a clear ground. $550

170 A festive sprig of black-tipped primroses with three buds is set over a clear grid-cut ground. $600

171 A red- and yellow-spotted black salamander on a multicolored jasper ground is placed next to a double pink clematis with upright stamens. The B signature cane is near the flower. $750

172 An elegant flower with buds of six different colors is set between deep green leaves. The red-over-white double overlay has been cut to resemble a basket. $2400

173 Enhanced by a gingham-cut green-over-white double overlay, a bouquet of six white flowers is set against a translucent ruby ground. $2000

174 This clear basket-cut weight contains a large lampwork flower with six small colorful buds and a ring of green leaves over a clear ground. $1800

175 A bouquet of blue and white pansies with tiny yellow upright stamens is set over a grid-cut base. Signed with a red, white and blue B cane at the base of the stems. (Bob Banford) $600

176 Two well-formed purple primroses with feathery upright yellow stamens and two small buds are set over a clear grid-cut base. (Bob Banford) $450

177 A single pink rose with two buds is enhanced by a clear star-cut base, one top facet, and six side facets. (Ray Banford) $600

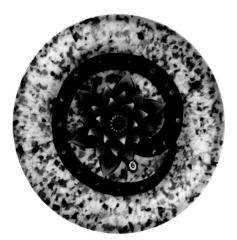

178 Set against an earth-like jasper ground, a black snake with red and yellow spots coils around a large red and blue lampwork flower. $650

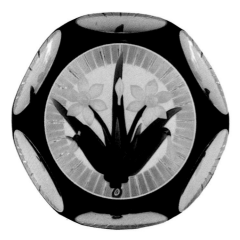

179 Two yellow daffodils with three unopened buds are encased in a green-over-white double overlay. The side facets reflect the spear cuts at the base of the overlay. $850

180 A brilliant array of complex lampwork flowers, each with a double row of petals and upright stamens, is set amidst branches and leaves over a clear grid-cut base. $2400

181 A trio of bright yellow daffodils with buds and long slender dark green leaves is set over a clear grid-cut base. (Bob Banford) $600

182 A bouquet of three irises, one red, one white and one blue, is set over a clear ground in this faceted weight. (Ray Banford) $600

183 A translucent cobalt blue ground and simple faceting complement a graceful sprig of lily-of-the-valley flowers. (Ray Banford) $450

184 A double red-over-white overlay encases a blue double clematis with upright yellow stamens and two delicate blue buds in different stages of bloom. (Bob Banford) $850

185 A bee and dragonfly, both with latticinio wings, hover over a colorful six-flower bouquet made up of a pansy and five flowers with double rows of petals. (Bob Banford) $2400

186 A yellow-over-white double overlay is cut to form a basket around a bouquet of royal blue iris. (Ray Banford) $1200

CORREIA

LOCATED ON THE PACIFIC COAST in Southern California, Correia Art Glass was founded in 1974 by glass artist Steven Correia. Nationally renowned, Correia Art Glass has been distinguished by commissions from the White House, the 1984 Olympic Committee, and the Metropolitan Museum of Art. Work from this studio is also included in the permanent collections of several museums including the Smithsonian Institution and the Corning Museum of Glass.

Correia is well known for unusual surface design paperweights and for a wide assortment of cut and faceted lampwork pieces. Chris Buzzini, who joined Correia in 1982, creates the lampwork pieces, which are characterized by exquisite three-dimensional floral, animal and aquatic scenes.

Correia Art Glass presents paperweight motifs in an unusual fashion. Each weight has a frosted outer surface with one large facet cut to reveal the interior design. Many of the motifs are set on richly colored grounds.

Each Correia Art Glass paperweight is signed, dated and accompanied by a certificate of authenticity.

187 An iridescent snake coils around a variegated golden globe in this unusual design. $110

188 A distinctively colored Monarch butterfly hovers over a spray of wild pink lupine in this delicate design surrounded by frosted sides. $160

189 A colorful red and blue songbird and a sprig of blue lupine are set against a dark ground. $160

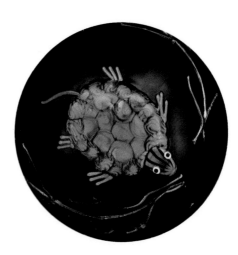

190 A green turtle and bare branches are fashioned in relief on the surface of this dark blue opaque weight. $90

191 A ruby-headed hummingbird sips nectar from pink trumpet flowers set on a dark translucent ground. $160

192 A spring bouquet of wildflowers set over a dark translucent ground is seen through a large top facet which is cut in the frosted globe. $160

D'ALBRET

IN 1967, PAUL JOKELSON, president of the Paperweight Collectors' Association, approached Cristalleries et Verreries de Viannes in Viannes, France with the idea of producing sulphide paperweights. In response to this suggestion, the glass company, which was founded in 1918 by Roger Witkind, inaugurated a series of sulphides under the name of "Cristalleries d'Albret."

Most of d'Albret's sulphides were designed and sculpted by Gilbert Poillerat, one of the best known and most prolific sulphide artists. Born in 1902, Poillerat studied decorative arts at the College Technique Boulle in Paris. Over the years he worked as a jewelry designer, a sculptor, and a professional medal engraver for the French Mint. In 1953, Poillerat, working in conjunction with Baccarat, was the artist responsible for producing the first successful modern sulphide. He continued to create dozens of exceptional pieces for Baccarat, Saint Louis, and Cristalleries d'Albret.

D'Albret sulphides are produced in both regular and overlay editions. All weights of the same subject are finished with identical faceting and the same color or color combinations. Weights are signed on the base with acid-etched letters arranged in a circle reading "CR. D'ALBRET—FRANCE." The cameo within the weight is signed on the edge of the bust with one or more of the following: the name of the subject, the date the sculpture was made, and the name or initials of the artist.

193 This unusual two-color sulphide in terra cotta and white celebrates the memory of Mahatma Gandhi. The cameo is set over a clear star-cut base with side finger facets. $100

194 From a sculpture by artist Leo Holmgren, this sulphide weight of H. M. Gustav VI, King of Sweden, is faceted and set over a translucent cobalt blue base. $70

195 A fancy-cut flash overlay highlights this sulphide of Albert Schweitzer, the renowned philosopher, missionary doctor and winner of the Nobel Peace Prize in 1952. The cameo is set over a clear star-cut ground. $185

CHARLES KAZIUN

CHARLES KAZIUN, one of the pioneers of modern paperweight making, has worked for almost fifty years rediscovering many of the lost techniques of the French glass factories of the nineteenth century. His work includes a wide range of millefiori, lampwork and crimped (Millville rose type) flower paperweights and related objects. He is also well known for double and triple overlays, miniature footed weights, and exquisite gold foil inclusions.

The beginning of Kaziun's career of experimentation and discovery in the field of glassblowing began when he was in the ninth grade and saw a family of glassblowers demonstrating ornamental lampworking at the county fair in his home town of Brockton, Massachusetts. Kaziun attended the fair daily, carefully observing the techniques of the lampworkers. He then went home and tried to duplicate what he had seen—using broken pieces of glass from bike taillights, Bromo-Seltzer bottles, and cold cream jars, heated over a crude Bunsen burner made from a coffee can.

After high school Kaziun developed his technical skills working in several different areas of scientific glassblowing. During that time an antique dealer asked him if he could copy an old glass paperweight-style button. Fascinated by the idea, Kaziun accepted the challenge.

Over the years Kaziun has developed a one-man method of millefiori cane production. He has also perfected a way of making fine muslin and swirling latticinio which he uses as grounds in his lampwork and millefiori weights.

Kaziun signs his weights with a 14K gold "K" and/or a millefiori "K" signature cane which is integrated into the design.

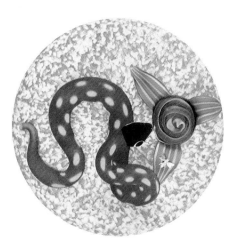

196 A gold foil bee rests on the leaves of a pink rose growing near an unusual red and yellow snake. The design is set on a beautifully colored blue and white jasper ground. $2600

197 This dramatic red and yellow striped snake is set over a dark ground covered by goldstone. $1200

198 This elegant weight contains an upright pink rose with four green leaves set in clear glass. $1000

199 A translucent amethyst ground enhances this blue and white striped morning glory with flowing stem and three green leaves. The weight is signed on the reverse with a gold foil K. $1200

200 This pansy with three millefiori lower petals and upright yellow stamens has a gold foil bee on one of the leaves and is set over a rose ground. $800

201 Surrounded by a pink and white ribbon twist torsade and set on a green goldstone ground, this patterned millefiori design includes a heart silhouette and a white stardust cane. Signed with a K cane on the torsade. $850

202 Set on a yellow ground, a large "Sunbonnet Sue" silhouette cane is surrounded by a two-tone pink torsade and six complex millefiori canes. $1700

203 In this miniature pedestal weight, a delicate upright spider lily is set over a colored goldstone ground. $395

204 A rich blue-over-white double overlay with one top facet and six side facets sets off a finely crafted bright yellow crimp rose. $4500

LUNDBERG STUDIOS

JAMES LUNDBERG, the founder of Lundberg Studios, studied glassworking at San Jose State University during the late 1960s. After graduating with a degree in art, and studying glass techniques throughout Europe, Lundberg joined several other artists and put together a small glass studio in San Jose, California.

In 1972, encouraged by L. H. Selman, Lundberg began applying some of his iridescent glass techniques and designs to paperweights. In 1973 Lundberg moved his operation to Davenport, California, a small town south of San Francisco, and set up a studio in a converted bakery.

Lundberg Studios is staffed by several artists, including Steven Lundberg and Daniel Salazar, who specialize in paperweight making. Steven Lundberg, a co-founder and co-owner of the business, trained as an apprentice with his brother James, and has worked in all aspects of glassmaking at Lundberg Studios. Daniel Salazar started as an apprentice at Lundberg Studios in 1975 and currently works making paperweights exclusively.

The artists at Lundberg Studios are well known for their iridescent art nouveau style paperweights, lamps, glassware and jewelry. They also produce very fine clear weights which include motifs such as flowers, birds, butterflies and seascapes. Some of their most recent paperweights contain three-dimensional flowers which are made by inserting motifs into the hot glass, rather than encasing them in crystal in the traditional manner. This technique allows for a spontaneous and flowing design.

James Lundberg, the mastermind behind many of the studio's new and innovative techniques, is responsible for developing all the glass and equipment used at Lundberg Studios. Paperweights produced by the studio are part of several major museum collections, including those of the Corning Museum of Glass, the Art Institute of Chicago, and the Smithsonian Institution.

Lundberg Studios paperweights are signed with the studio name, artist's name, date and number. Since July 1980 all Lundberg pieces have been accompanied by a certificate of authenticity.

205 A delicate many-petaled mauve peony with green leaves and upright millefiori stamens is set over a clear ground. $220

206 A realistic snow-white gardenia with green leaves is set against a cobalt blue ground. $180

207 This bouquet, made up of brilliant yellow sundrops with millefiori stamens and green leaves, is set over a clear ground. $220

208 Two well-formed pink azaleas with upright stamens and deeply veined cupped green leaves are set over a clear ground. $200

209 A trio of pink phlox with delicately formed yellow upright stamens and green leaves is enhanced by a white jasper ground. $200

210 A deep blue iridescent ground makes up the backdrop for this underwater world with a tropical fish and a school of jellyfish swimming through a pale green kelp forest. $180

211 This full pink dahlia with deeply veined petals on a bed of green leaves is reminiscent of a classic Saint Louis design. $200

212 A realistic upright tiger lily with spotted petals and deep green leaves is the subject of this pedestal weight. $200

213 Silhouetted against a full moon and midnight sky, a majestic great blue heron sits in a blossoming cherry tree. $180

MICHAEL O'KEEFE

WORKING IN A CONVERTED storefront in Seattle's south end, glass artist Michael O'Keefe is creating a new and exciting look in paperweights. O'Keefe's distinctive weights feature three-dimensional translucent forms in a range of soft colors. The exterior shape of each piece is specially designed to complement the interior motif.

O'Keefe began learning about glass while studying at the Center for Creative Studies in Detroit, where he received his BFA in photography. After graduating in 1976 he worked at the Poultry Glassworks in downtown Detroit, where he first became familiar with paperweight making.

At Poultry Glassworks O'Keefe learned the silver veiling technique which he uses in creating his paperweights. Silver veiling involves the melting together of silver and glass. By reheating the glass the silver is drawn to the surface where the design is developed. Then additional glass encases the design and the outside is fire polished.

The unusually subtle and delicate colors in O'Keefe's weights are due to the ingredients he uses in his glass mixture. Certain elements in the formula cause the silver to react in specific ways. When the glass is pulled and twisted, the silver causes the glass to change color—sometimes from brown to yellow, or from yellow to blue. Another factor which controls the color is the rate at which the glass is reheated and cooled.

Although his pieces involve sophisticated technology and a high degree of craftsmanship, O'Keefe manages to maintain an overall feeling of simplicity and elegance in his work. Each piece is engraved on the bottom with the artist's name and the date.

MICHAEL O'KEEFE

214 This spiral design, reminiscent of the inside swirl of a seashell, is formed in pale blue glass by the process of silver veiling. $100

215 In this weight the same silver veiled design as above is executed in amber glass. $100

216 Blue glass and silver veiling are combined in this fan-shaped spiral design, which is also available in amber glass. $100

ORIENT & FLUME

IN 1972 DOUGLAS BOYD and David Hopper opened a small glassblowing studio on the corner of Orient and Flume Streets in Chico, California. The two artists, who had taken part in some of the earliest college classes offered in glassblowing on the west coast, received master's degrees in glass from California State University in San Jose. After graduation the two traveled extensively, studying antique glass and glassmaking techniques in many parts of the world.

Today Orient & Flume has grown to include a staff of twenty people. They describe themselves as both a studio and a factory in that they have the size to dependably produce glass in quantity, yet are small enough to allow each person to work and create as an individual.

Orient & Flume successfully synthesizes glass styles and techniques from many different time periods and parts of the world and adds to these their own contemporary artistic interpretations. The company developed its reputation producing brilliant iridescent glass paperweights with art nouveau motifs and elaborate surface decoration. Their latest weights combine these elements with traditional paperweight designs and techniques. Most are clear-encased rather than surface designs.

Orient & Flume paperweights are signed, dated, and numbered on the base. Each piece is issued with a certificate of authenticity.

217 A Canada goose swims through a cluster of swaying reeds. $150

218 A ruby-throated hummingbird hovering near a branch of pink dogwood is set over a clear ground. $175

219 A garden-fresh arrangement of a white calla lily, bird-of-paradise, and sprigs of blue knotweed is set over a clear ground. $175

220 A brilliant bird-of-paradise blossom fills this clear-encased weight. $150

221 A black and white spotted loon swims through blue water with green reeds, set over a clear ground.　　$175

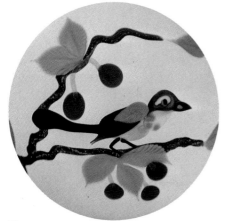

222 A blue jay in a cherry tree adorns the surface of this frosted weight.　　$125

223 Set against a deep blue ground, a mallard duck descends on a pond with green and brown cattails. $175

224 Two delicate yellow daffodils with slender green leaves are depicted on this surface-design weight with a black background. $100

225 A turquoise, blue and red millefiori butterfly hovers over a translucent white morning glory and bud set over a clear ground. $175

226 A brown thrasher sits on a yellow flowering desert cactus over an iridescent pale ground. $150

227 Three graceful fireflowers on a vine with deeply veined leaves are set over a clear ground. $200

228 Two bright red wild roses with a bud and green leaves are set over a clear ground with allover side faceting. $350

PARABELLE GLASS

GARY SCRUTTON and his wife Doris, of Parabelle Glass, are the only studio artists in this country concentrating exclusively on the production of millefiori paperweights. Working in a small studio in back of their home in Portland, Oregon, the Scruttons produce their own glass and develop their own colors. Their classic-style paperweights encompass a wide range of designs including close packed millefiori, garlands, and stave basket weights.

Gary Scrutton began working in glass more than forty years ago. He trained as an apprentice after high school, learning general glassworking techniques such as bevelling, etching, and mirror silvering. In 1972 he started his own studio which specialized in stained glass, and crystal and glass repair. Scrutton sold his successful Portland-based business to his sons in 1983. It was then that Gary and Doris started Parabelle Glass and began concentrating on paperweight making.

With only the most general information available, Gary set out to solve the mysteries of millefiori paperweight production. He encountered a host of problems involving equipment, colors, cane making, and design. One of the biggest challenges was learning how to heat the arrangement of canes in such a way that the spaces fused together without trapping air. After a year of experimentation, he succeeded.

Doris, who creates some of the paperweight designs, also helps Gary stretch the millefiori canes. In the traditional manner, pontil rods are attached to each end of a thick heated cane and then quickly stretched to a length of forty to a hundred feet. The "walker" must walk or run according to how hot the glass is and what diameter cane is being produced.

The Scruttons' studio is highly sophisticated; their equipment includes heat exchangers and other fuel-saving devices. A computer operates the main furnace, which holds two large hooded pots for melting crystal and two smaller pots for colored glass.

Parabelle weights include a cane with the initials "PG" and the year.

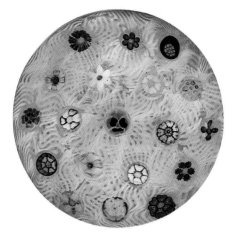

229 This classic-style scattered mille-fiori lace design has a pansy cane at the center, a white and green Clichy-type rose, and an edelweiss cane. $150

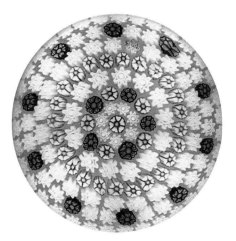

230 This well-designed concentric millefiori weight in shades of blue and white is signed PG1986 in a cane. $120

231 A blue and white stave basket sur-rounds a close packed millefiori design which displays a variety of canes, includ-ing Clichy-type rose and edelweiss canes. $185

232 A red rooster silhouette is the center cane in this concentric millefiori weight which also contains a ring of edelweiss canes and a blue and white torsade. $140

233 Complex millefiori garlands of purple and blue intertwine in this beautifully designed weight which includes seven white and green Clichy-type roses. $180

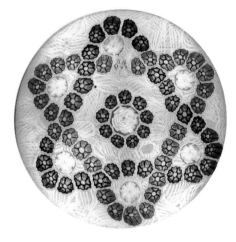

234 Animal silhouettes form the centers of seven circles of complex millefiori canes set on upset muslin. $160

PERTHSHIRE PAPERWEIGHTS

PERTHSHIRE PAPERWEIGHTS, located in Crieff, Scotland, was established in 1968 by Stuart Drysdale, a country lawyer and businessman. Drysdale, who first became familiar with paperweight manufacture while managing Vasart Glass and Strathearn Glass, was introduced to the beauty and technical sophistication of antique French paperweights through an article in an American magazine in 1967. He became fascinated with the idea of rediscovering nineteenth-century paperweight making techniques and with creating a glass factory devoted to the production of classic-style millefiori and lampwork paperweights.

In the tradition of the great nineteenth-century glass factories of France, the craftsmen at Perthshire work together as a team designing and producing paperweights. Millefiori designs are created by the glassworkers themselves and experimentation is encouraged.

About three-quarters of a ton of glass is produced each week at Perthshire. The basic ingredient of the factory's high quality "metal" (glass) is white sand from northwest Scotland.

Each year Perthshire issues a special collection of paperweights which are produced only that year in a limited edition. These yearly limited editions include a cane containing the "P" signature, or a "P" cane with the year of issue.

Perthshire also produces paperweights in regular limited editions which are repeated each year in small numbers, and a number of designs which are not designated as limited. All of these weights are signed with either a single "P" cane within the design, or a "P" cane and the year of manufacture located within the motif or on the base of the weight. Some of these are marked with a cane containing a letter of the alphabet—"A" representing 1969 (the first year of production) through "R" representing 1986.

235 A pale blue and white primrose with millefiori stamens and five buds is set on white latticinio in this 1984 special limited edition weight. Also available with a pink flower. $350

236 A finely crafted yellow double clematis with cupped petals and millefiori stamens is set at the center of a blue crown with goldstone thread twists. 1984 special limited edition. $395

237 A pale green silkworm crawls across two mulberry leaves set over a clear ground in this faceted weight. 1984 special limited edition. $240

238 One in a series of innovative hollow weights, this 1984 special limited edition contains a brown lampwork squirrel and has an amber flash overlay. Cut with vertical flutes. $500

239 A pink and white dahlia with two rows of petals is placed on a fountain of leaves in this clear faceted weight. Special limited edition, 1985. $375

240 A bouquet of three pink primroses is displayed in a flowerpot, bordered by a ring of millefiori canes, and set on a brilliant blue ground. Cane and flowerpot colors vary in this 1984 special limited edition. $200

241 Set on a translucent ruby ground, a beautiful millefiori heart is surrounded by a single ring of canes which appears double when viewed through the top facet (PP46). $125

242 A blue, white, and pink triple overlay encases a blue and white bouquet set over a clear grid-cut base. Special limited edition, 1985. $450

243 Three fancy-petal primroses with millefiori centers are surrounded by a border of complex canes set in clear glass and faceted. Colors vary in this 1985 special limited edition. $300

244 A dark green translucent ground complements a sprig of deep yellow Scotch broom. This 1985 special limited edition has top and side faceting. $375

245 Three lampwork ducks swim in a blue pond in this hollow faceted weight. This special limited edition has an apple-green flash overlay and is signed P1983 in a cane on the base. $480

246 Surrounded by two rings of mille-fiori canes, a bold lampwork flower with unusual latticinio twist petals is set in clear glass on a translucent ground and faceted. Colors vary in this 1984 special limited edition. $225

247 Black, pink and pistachio twists radiate from a central complex cane in this 1971 special limited edition crown weight. $300

248 A patterned millefiori design, which includes a variety of complex canes and sections of lace twists, is set on a color cushion ground. Colors vary in this 1971 special limited edition. $185

249 This encased overlay weight, which is part of a special series featuring state birds, includes a finely crafted silhouette cane surrounded by a concentric millefiori border. Prices vary. $1200

250 A miniature weight displaying patterned millefiori is set on a translucent color ground. The colors vary in this yearly limited edition (PP63); the design is exclusive to 1985. $82.50

251 Set on a white upset muslin ground, this patterned millefiori design with cane twists has a thistle picture cane at the center (PP27). $150

252 Designed around a central P signature cane, this concentric millefiori weight with fluted sides is set over a dark blue ground. Millefiori cane colors vary (PP53). $55

253 A spray of lampwork flowers and buds with a millefiori and cane twist border are set over a translucent color ground. The ground colors vary in this 1986 special limited edition. $350

254 A picture cane of a candle surrounded by holly is the center of this festive red, white and green Christmas crown weight. Special limited edition, 1985. $350

255 This miniature concentric millefiori weight is set on an opaque ground and signed in the center with a P cane. Colors vary (PP3). $25

256 An array of finely crafted complex canes makes up this close packed millefiori weight, a 1986 special limited edition. $225

257 Close concentric rings of millefiori are divided into a star pattern by lengthwise sections of millefiori canes. A yearly limited edition (PP85). $160

258 Four tiers of petals make up this large mustard yellow dahlia with a P signature cane at the center. Cut with one top facet and five side facets, this weight is a 1986 special limited edition. $550

259 A golfer in full swing, formed by the glass transfer technique, is set on upset muslin with a millefiori and cane twist border. Colors vary (PP81). $160

260 A lively pattern of millefiori canes and ribbon twists surrounds a glass transfer locomotive set on lace. Colors vary (PP56). $160

261 Signed in the center with a P cane, this patterned millefiori weight is made with varying designs, millefiori, and ground colors (PP5). $55

262 A Perthshire signature cane is surrounded by four picture canes of animals
in this spaced millefiori design set on
mauve lace. A 1985 yearly limited edition. $95

263 An arrangement of lampwork
flowers with large ribbed petals and
green leaves on a dark blue ground
makes up this 1986 special limited edition. $300

264 Bordered by millefiori canes of alternating colors, this spaced millefiori
on lace includes four picture canes of
animals. The animal canes and colors
vary in this yearly limited edition. $155

KEN ROSENFELD

BASED IN LOS ANGELES, paperweight artist Ken Rosenfeld creates beautifully detailed lampwork designs in the traditional French style. His weights include a variety of single flowers, bouquets, and fruit arrangements, as well as a "vegetable garden" weight.

Rosenfeld, who has a master's degree in fine arts from Southern Illinois University, first became interested in glass while studying ceramics in graduate school. After college he returned to his native California and, with a partner, started a small glass studio. While working as a scientific glassblower he became familiar with sophisticated glass technology and advanced techniques in the field.

It was at the 1980 Paperweight Collectors' Association convention in New York City that Rosenfeld encountered his first paperweights. The displays of exquisite antique French weights and the collections of extraordinary pieces created by contemporary artists inspired Rosenfeld to turn his attention toward paperweight making.

Rosenfeld's work reflects his skill as a master craftsman as well as his accomplishments as an artist and designer. His use of color is especially sophisticated and gives his weights a distinctive brilliance.

Rosenfeld's paperweights are signed with an "R" cane, and his name and the date are engraved on the base of each piece.

265 Three ripe strawberries, a blossom and leaves are set over a clear diamond-cut base. $275

266 A delicate carpet of blue and white lampwork flowers forms the ground for four large multicolored blooms. $275

267 A well-formed pink cabbage rose and bud are set on a stem with green leaves over a clear ground. $200

268 This splendid multicolored bouquet with feathery upright stamens and five buds is enhanced by a clear diamond-cut base. $300

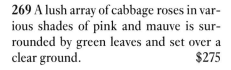

269 A lush array of cabbage roses in various shades of pink and mauve is surrounded by green leaves and set over a clear ground. $275

270 Brightly colored garden-fresh carrots, radishes, turnips and asparagus make up this unusual vegetable bouquet set in clear glass. $200

271 This richly colored fruit weight includes a cluster of cherries, a pear, and two plums with green leaves over a clear ground. $250

272 Three beautifully crafted lampwork flowers form this upright bouquet with deep green leaves set over a clear ground. $200

273 A bouquet made up of two pink cabbage roses, three clematis flowers, and a ripe strawberry with a white blossom is set over a clear ground. $300

MODERN SAINT LOUIS

IN 1953, AFTER A LAPSE of eighty-six years, Cristalleries de Saint Louis once again began to produce paperweights. At that time Paul Gossman, an energetic young glassmaker at Saint Louis, consulted with the older workers at the factory and conducted test after test to rediscover the forgotten millefiori, lampwork, and sulphide paperweight making techniques. Although his experiments led to the making of some weights during the next few years, it was not until 1970 that Saint Louis began producing quality weights on a regular basis.

Each year Saint Louis creates an outstanding collection of limited edition paperweights. Many of the millefiori and lampwork designs in these pieces are fashioned after superb nineteenth-century designs. Saint Louis specializes in a variety of paperweight styles and techniques including the production of mushroom weights, piedouches, upright bouquets, and magnum encased double overlays. The company also produces a number of paperweight related objects such as handcoolers, candlesticks, newel posts, and penholders.

Modern Saint Louis paperweights contain a cane with the date and the initials "SL". Each weight is produced as part of a limited edition and is accompanied by a certificate of authenticity.

274 A dazzling honeycomb pattern of complex millefiori canes is set off by a royal blue cushion ground. A 1984 limited edition weight. $540

275 Deep colored plums on a stem with serrated leaves are set against a white ground. Limited edition, 1984. $400

276 A 24-karat gold foil inclusion of King Tutankhamen, fashioned from a medal by Arthus Bertrand Co., Paris, is surrounded by a ring of millefiori canes on an opaque orange or turquoise ground. Limited edition, 1979. $490

277 Finely detailed white clematis with red tipped petals and complex millefiori stamens are set over a pale blue latticinio ground. Limited edition, 1985. $400

278 A royal blue opaque ground provides a backdrop for a sprig of bright red holly with scalloped leaves. $380

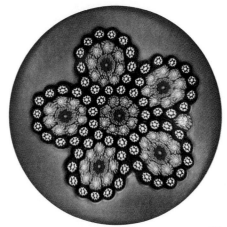

279 A complex millefiori doily pattern is set on a dark orange cushion ground in this 1984 limited edition. $540

280 This colorful bouquet, made up of several different lampwork flowers, includes an SL1981 signature cane in the center of a white bloom. $560

281 Resembling an antique Baccarat weight in design, color and craftsmanship, this superb bouquet has red, white and blue flowers with stamens of stardust cane clusters set over a clear ground. Limited edition, 1986. $490

282 Multicolored fruit, including cherries, plums, and pears, rest on a latticinio ground in this pedestal weight fashioned after a classic Saint Louis design. Limited edition, 1985. $600

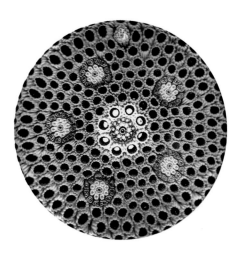

283 A magnificent carpet ground of green and blue hollow canes provides the backdrop for five pastel complex canes surrounding a large complex center cane. This weight is signed SL 1986 in a pink and white cane near the edge of the weight. $440

284 Closely resembling an antique Baccarat gentian flower, this weight has three white-edged amber flowers with a bud and green leaves set over a clear ground. Limited edition, 1986. $380

285 A delicate spray of tiny red-tipped bellflowers is set on a blue ground. This 1986 limited edition has one top facet and six side facets. $400

286 In this miniature weight a pale pink primrose with a bud and green leaves is set against an opaque sky blue ground. Signed SL1986 in the center of the flower, it is a limited edition. $300

287 Entitled "Amour," this weight combines several paperweight styles and techniques; a well-crafted sulphide of Cupid is surrounded by blue lampwork forget-me-nots with millefiori cane centers and set on a brilliant encased pink-red color ground. Limited edition of 400. $385

288 Created in commemoration of the coronation of Queen Elizabeth II in 1953, this finely crafted sulphide is made in several different ground colors, faceting patterns and millefiori colors. $350

DAVID SALAZAR

IN 1972, WHILE ATTENDING San Jose State University in California, David Salazar began working with glass as an apprentice at Lundberg Studios. He immediately fell in love with glass-making and found himself particularly fascinated by the design process. Paperweights proved to be the perfect format for his skills and ideas.

Salazar has been producing paperweights on his own for the past few years, and recently built a new studio in Santa Cruz, California. The workshop includes two furnaces which can accommodate several pots. This setup allows him to work with a number of different colors at a time. He has assisted other glassworkers in constructing studios, and found creating one on his own to be an exciting challenge. The project has given him the opportunity to create a work environment which is clean, well-organized and energy-efficient.

Salazar produces weights with colorful floral and classic motifs. Many of his newest pieces are miniatures with elegant and well-executed surface designs. He has also created a marbrie weight fashioned after the classic Saint Louis design.

All Salazar weights are signed and dated on the base.

289 This marbrie weight has a swirling red, white and green surface design with a starry cane center. Made in both miniature and regular size:

Miniature:	$55
Regular:	$75

290 A graceful blue butterfly hovers near pink wildflowers on the white surface of this opaque weight. Made in three sizes:

Miniature:	$45
Medium:	$65
Regular:	$90

291 This surface-decorated weight displays a golden crescent moon and brilliant white stars in a night sky. Made in two sizes:

Miniature:	$45
Medium:	$60

JAMES SHAW

A NATIVE CALIFORNIAN, James Shaw began his artistic career as a ceramicist. In 1976, James Lundberg offered Shaw a place to fire his kiln—Lundberg Glass Studios. It was only a matter of time before Shaw, curious about the work that was going on all around him, dropped ceramics and began working in glass.

Shaw was particularly interested in the delicate grinding and polishing process which is so important in paperweight making. After several years of refining his skills in this area, he began concentrating on paperweight conservation and restoration. Since 1978 Shaw has worked on nearly a thousand paperweights, sensitively repairing damage and restoring pieces to their original shapes and faceting patterns.

Recently Shaw has started producing his own paperweights. The style of his work and the geometric shapes of his pieces grew out of his extensive sculpting, cutting and faceting experience. In both his ceramics and his paperweight restoration work, Shaw found himself limited to creating and preserving round shapes. His paperweights break through this limitation and open up an entirely new world of design and creativity.

Shaw signs his paperweights with the initials "JAS" and the year in script on the side.

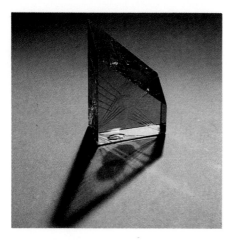

292 Mauve neodymium glass is faceted with four sets of fan cuts and concave circles. The color of the glass, which changes with the light source, ranges from pale purple to deep rose. $350

293 This richly colored triangular sculpture is made of cobalt blue boron crystal cut with thin diagonal lines and concave circles. $255

294 A striking three-dimensional effect is created within this four-sided sculpture where the lines of the side and bottom facets join in a triangle. The lead content of the pale amber crystal in this weight is 45%. $185

GORDON SMITH

GORDON SMITH, a talented young paperweight artist from New Jersey, first became interested in glass at the age of fourteen when his father brought him a melting torch and some scrap glass. After graduation from high school, Smith studied glass at Salem Community College and then began work in the scientific glassblowing industry.

Smith was introduced to paperweight making through the work of Jim and Nontas Kontes, while working for Kontes Scientific Glass. The Kontes brothers encouraged Smith to pursue his fascination with paperweights, and told the young artist about the extensive paperweight collection at Wheaton Museum of American Glass. Eventually Smith became a weekend volunteer at the glass factory at Wheaton Village, where he spent time learning more about paperweight making and developing his own techniques.

Although Smith has received help and encouragement from a number of accomplished paperweight artists such as the Kontes brothers, Bob Banford, and Paul Stankard, he has had to work hard to discover for himself many of the closely guarded secrets of the profession. His paperweights reflect a knowledge and understanding of classic lampwork paperweight making techniques as well as a creative design approach.

Smith signs his paperweights on the side with etched initials "GES" and the year.

295 Three delicate white bellflowers growing on a vine with curled green leaves are set against a translucent cobalt blue ground. $450

296 A graceful and well-formed lady's-slipper orchid with long slender leaves is set over a clear ground. $325

297 A tropical bird-of-paradise flower is framed by a dark ground. $350

298 Realistic strawberries with a single white blossom are set against a rich cobalt blue ground. $500

299 A beautiful orchid and bud are set in clear glass over a dark blue translucent ground. $325

300 A pale yellow orchid with speckled labellum and variegated leaves is set over a clear ground. $325

PAUL STANKARD

PAUL STANKARD, of Mantua, New Jersey, has worked for more than fifteen years expanding both the technical and artistic limits of paperweight making. Stankard's unparalleled floral weights, his innovative "botanicals," and his most recent "environmental" paperweights, reflect his skills both as a master craftsman and creative artist.

Stankard developed his knowledge and expertise working as a scientific glassblower for ten years. His experience with sophisticated glassmaking technology has helped him to achieve the precision and control which are critical to his goals as a maker.

While working as a scientific glassblower, Stankard became interested in antique French paperweights. The Ware Collection of Blaschka glass plant models on display at the Peabody Botanical Museum at Harvard University led to his fascination with glass flowers.

An amateur botanist as well as a paperweight artist, Stankard uses his extensive knowledge of the plant world to make accurate and naturalistic reproductions in glass. Each detail of his pieces—design, color, construction—is carefully planned and executed. Stankard makes sketches from nature and examines fresh flowers as he creates his glass pieces. Many of his weights contain intricate root systems which are detailed with as much care and precision as the colorful blooms above ground.

Stankard's early weights bear an etched signature on the base or side of the piece, or include an "S" or "PS" signature cane. His recent work contains an "S" signature cane. Many of Stankard's weights are one-of-a-kind pieces or variations on a particular theme. Colors and details within each weight are slightly different. If you wish information about specific weights please call or write us. We will be happy to send you color Polaroids of weights in stock.

301 Pale pink morning glories with yellow stamens grow on a curling stem with tendrils and arrow-shaped leaves. The arrangement is set on a translucent cobalt blue ground. $1000

302 Two epiphytic orchids grow on a tree branch set over a pale translucent amethyst ground. $1000

303 Attached to a lichen-covered tree branch, a pale yellow epiphytic orchid with orange spots is set over a clear ground. $1000

304 A branch with three deep red raspberries, white blossoms with yellow stamens, and two buds is set over a clear ground. $800

305 A red opaque ground provides the backdrop for a yellow flowering desert cactus with an exposed root system and three fruit. $1000

306 A pale yellow orchid plant with long green leaves and exposed roots is enhanced by a rich red ground. $800

307 This delicate plant with pale blue blossoms is shown with intricately crafted roots and bulb set over a clear ground. $850

308 A stem of blue morning glories with white stripes and arrow-shaped leaves is set on a pale green ground. $1000

309 Pale pink trailing arbutus flowers are surrounded by realistic leaves over a clear ground. $850

310 A multicolored bouquet of pink trailing arbutus, blue forget-me-nots, and red bellflowers, with leaves of each plant, is set over a clear ground. $1500

311 A realistic black and yellow honeybee pollinates a pale pink daisy. Set over a clear ground. $850

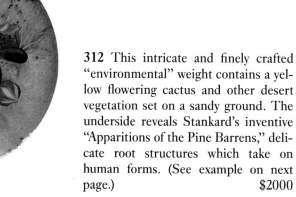

312 This intricate and finely crafted "environmental" weight contains a yellow flowering cactus and other desert vegetation set on a sandy ground. The underside reveals Stankard's inventive "Apparitions of the Pine Barrens," delicate root structures which take on human forms. (See example on next page.) $2000

313 A trailing arbutus grows on a richly detailed forest floor with "Apparitions of the Pine Barrens" on the underside of the weight. $1500

314 This weight illustrates the fascinating imaginative realm Stankard has created on the underside of many of his botanical weights. Several of these weights were inspired by the ecologically rich pine barren region near the artist's home. $1500

315 An orange desert flower is set on a rich sandy ground with anthropomorphic root structures on the underside of the weight. $1500

DELMO AND DEBBIE TARSITANO

DELMO AND DEBBIE TARSITANO, father and daughter, will soon be celebrating their tenth anniversary as paperweight artists. The Tarsitanos began collecting antique paperweights in 1971. Enthusiasm for the objects combined with an interest in experimentation led to their first paperweight making success in 1976. Since that time the two artists have worked originating their own designs and assisting each other in the paperweight making process.

Delmo is currently working on large salamander weights. He is also developing an idea which he calls "earth-life"—weights which display animals and insects in their natural environment. These pieces contain rocks, flowers, and skillfully designed plants set in a realistic earth ground.

Debbie, who now lives in Massachusetts, has developed a lampworking studio in her home where she creates her paperweight designs and set-ups. She frequently commutes to her father's studio on Long Island, where she encases her pieces. The design and perspective of Debbie's latest work have been greatly influenced by her study of painting. Her pieces include detailed bouquets, some of which contain flowers with silhouette canes incorporated into the stamens. Debbie is also producing a number of paperweights with the glass engraver Max Erlacher. These pieces set Debbie's beautifully crafted lampwork flowers and plants against Erlacher's engraved background scenes.

Tarsitano paperweights are produced in small editions. Until 1980, their weights were signed with an initial "T" cane. Currently their pieces are identified by a "DT" cane. Since Delmo is now making some floral weights too, he plans to change his signature cane to "AT" (for Adelmo Tarsitano) so the two Tarsitanos can be identified.

316 This well-formed many-petaled pink rose is surrounded by classic green leaves and set over a clear star-cut base. The weight is signed with a DT cane at the base of the stem. $780

317 A colorful patch of garden primroses and pansies attracts a black and yellow honeybee set over a clear ground. $900

318 Two beautiful purple clematis with Clichy-type roses at the center and three sprigs of blue knotweed are set over a clear ground. $850

319 A border of blue ribbons surrounds a bouquet of three pink flowers with yellow-sided petals and millefiori stamens. Cut with allover side faceting and set over a clear star-cut base. $950

320 An elegant bouquet of pink and blue daylilies with slender green leaves is set over a clear ground. $650

321 Inspired by a walk through the New England countryside, this "woodwalk" bouquet contains a variety of brightly colored summer blooms surrounded by leaves and fresh green grass. $1500

322 A country scene designed by Debbie Tarsitano and engraved on the base of the weight by Max Erlacher is enhanced by a lush field of Debbie's colorful lampwork flowers and grasses. The scene is surrounded by diamond-faceted sides and set in clear glass. (Photographed on a black background.) $2600

323 Brilliant sunflowers with large upright camomile millefiori centers and two sprigs of blue knotweed are set over a clear ground. $570

324 A wild red rose with yellow upright stamens and a rose hip is encased in clear glass and faceted. The base is star-cut. $600

325 A graceful hummingbird, designed by Debbie Tarsitano and engraved by Max Erlacher, hovers within a wreath of pansies, white knotweed and lily-of-the-valley tied with a blue ribbon. $1200

326 A wreath of purple lampwork flowers with yellow upright stamens surrounds two frolicking unicorns engraved by Max Erlacher. $1850

327 Three red and white primroses form a brilliant garland over Max Erlacher's engraving of a swan swimming in a lily pond with cattails. $1700

328 A well-crafted salamander with brown latticinio back and legs is set on a sandy ground with an upright blue flower. $1800

329 A lush red strawberry with two snow-white blossoms is set over a clear star-cut base with faceted sides. $700

330 A spider in its nest and a stem of yellow morning glories are set on a rich sandy ground. $900

331 Two sky-blue morning glories with long yellow stamens, a bud and leaves are set over a clear star-cut ground. $675

332 Set on a sandy ground, a finely crafted spider lurks near a fruiting strawberry plant. $1200

333 A vivid red salamander with black spots rests on a large purple dahlia. Signed near the edge with a DT cane and set on a sandy ground. $1500

VICTOR TRABUCCO

VICTOR TRABUCCO, who lives in Buffalo, New York, has been creating classic-style lampwork paperweights since 1977. His beautifully crafted flowers, bouquets, fruit, and animals have greatly contributed to the paperweight renaissance.

Trabucco's interest in glass began in 1974 when he first saw a lampworking demonstration. Soon after, he began working with the medium and developing his skills as a glass sculptor. His sculptures, many of which were commissioned by large corporations, were very well received, and several of his pieces received awards of merit. Trabucco became intrigued with the idea of paperweight making after examining a collection of nineteenth-century French paperweights. After a year and a half of hard work and experimentation he mastered the technique. He found the paperweight format exciting and the ultimate challenge for himself as a glass artist.

Trabucco has recently started producing magnum size weights which are four inches and five inches in diameter. Inspired by Mount Washington and Pantin, the flowers in these pieces, which are extremely full and three-dimensional, appear even larger and more dramatic because of the magnification through the added crystal .

Trabucco is the first American studio artist to eliminate the seam or division line which usually occurs in the glass of lampwork weights. As a result of this significant technical achievement, Trabucco's weights can be viewed from the side as well as the top with no obstruction.

Trabucco's weights usually include a "T" or "VT" cane, and his signature and the date are engraved on the side of each piece.

334 A translucent cobalt blue ground serves as a backdrop for this brilliant red rose surrounded by four buds and green leaves. $400

335 This magnum weight has a delicate pink camellia and buds set over a translucent cobalt blue ground. $600

336 Elegant pink orchids are set over a cobalt blue translucent ground in this beautiful magnum weight. $750

337 Two-color daffodils, purple violets and buds make up this attractive bouquet set over a sky-blue ground. $450

338 In this magnum weight a bouquet made with a full red rose, three pink wild roses, and sprigs of white knotweed is set over a sky-blue ground. $800

339 This magnum weight contains two red strawberries with blossom, buds and green leaves over a blue ground. $750

340 Larger than magnum size, this super-magnum weight contains a bouquet made up of a camellia, buttercups, morning glory, and violets over a clear ground. $2500

341 A superb bouquet with a pastel pink camellia, blue morning glories, white knotweed and purple bellflowers is set over a clear ground in this super-magnum weight. $2000

342 A multicolored bouquet, set in a magnum weight over a clear ground, includes a pink rose, spring beauty, buttercups, and morning glories. $800

343 In this magnum weight two full pink roses with buds and sprigs of white knotweed are set off by a brilliant cobalt blue ground. $800

344 A branch with rose-colored camellia blossoms and buds is set over a sky-blue ground. $400

345 A vivid yellow convolvulus flower and bud are placed on a graceful stem with green leaves and tendrils over a dark blue ground. $375

PAUL YSART

Born in Barcelona, Spain in 1904, Paul Ysart is considered one of the most important contributors to twentieth-century paperweight making. Active since the 1930s, Ysart was one of the first contemporary craftsmen to rediscover and refine paperweight making techniques.

Both Ysart's father Salvador and his grandfather were glassblowers in Spain. Just prior to World War I Salvador moved his family to France, where he continued to improve his skills as a master glassworker. In 1915 the family moved to Scotland, where Salvador was employed by Leith Flint Glassworks in Edinburgh. It was there at the age of thirteen that Paul, Salvador's oldest son, began training as his father's servitor. In 1922 Salvador was offered a position at Moncrieff Glassworks in Perth, Scotland, and he brought along Paul and his other three sons as apprentice glassblowers. Here Paul, with the help of his family, began experimenting with paperweight making.

By 1938 Paul Ysart was creating quality paperweights, some of which were marketed by Moncrieff Glassworks. Although his brothers branched off and created their own glassworks, Paul remained with Moncrieff until 1963, when he went to work at Caithness Glass in Wick, Scotland. In 1971, Ysart started the Paul Ysart Glass Company in Wick, which specialized in paperweights and other glass objects produced in limited editions. He retired in 1979. Over nearly fifty years of paperweight making, Ysart produced a wide range of millefiori designs set on clear, colored and lace grounds. He is also known for his well-crafted lampwork motifs including flowers, butterflies, lacy and decorated snakes, dragonflies, and swimming fish.

Most paperweights made by Ysart contain a small "PY" signature cane either in the design or on the base of the piece.

346 Set on an opaque mauve ground, this colorful lampwork bouquet has a large red flower in the center. Signed PY in a cane under the central flower. $650

347 A dragonfly with millefiori wings and a goldstone yellow spotted body is surrounded by millefiori canes and set against a dark ground. Signed with a PY cane near the insect's tail. $700

348 A millefiori-winged butterfly is encircled by a complementary millefiori cane border and set on an opaque pink ground. $700

349 This insculpture weight by Vander-mark-Merritt has an orchid cut into the center and a ring of pink and white orchids around the outside made using the diatreta technique. The outer flowers are carefully cut away from layers of green, white and pink glass to capture the orchid's subtle color variations. There are several different flowers in this series. $3000

350 A *dua flora* surface design on this weight by David Lotton is enhanced by iridescent frost. $125

351 The Star of David is surrounded by lavish concentric circles of blue and white millefiori canes in this Whitefriars weight, issued for the thirtieth anniversary of the State of Israel and dated 1978 in a cane within the design. (Weights signed "Whitefriars" and dated later than 1981 are products of the Caithness glass factory, which purchased the rights to the 300-year-old Whitefriars name when the factory closed in 1981.) Limited edition. $195

352 Two lampwork blooms and a sprig of millefiori flowers make up this delicate bouquet set over a clear ground. Signed with a W cane in the center of the pink flower. $320

353 Blue bellflowers with green leaves are set against a translucent garnet ground. A signature cane is included near the base of the stem. $350

354 A purple and pink fuchsia hangs from a stem with a bud and three leaves over a translucent green ground. $400

355 Surrounded by a garland of blue and white canes, a millefiori butterfly on a purple ground is encased in clear glass and cut with thumbprint facets. $325

356 A radiant red and white primrose with a bud is encircled by a ring of alternating purple and white canes set in clear glass and faceted. $240

357 A graceful latticinio-winged dragonfly is set over purple and white primroses in this faceted clear weight. $325

PAPERWEIGHT RELATED OBJECTS

358 This very delicate antique Baccarat footed goblet is decorated with thin slices of millefiori canes and starburst cutting. $1200

359 Close packed millefiori canes against a cobalt blue ground make up the base and stopper of this faceted inkwell by Perthshire Paperweights. $350

360 This "nature in ice" sculpture by Victor Trabucco includes brilliant lampwork Ming roses. $600

361 Concentric rings of millefiori set on a translucent color ground form the base of this Perthshire perfume bottle with encased glass thread stopper. Signed in the center of the base with a P cane. Colors vary. $110

362 Close packed millefiori on a dark blue ground make up this elegant Perthshire doorknob with brass fittings. $90

363 This miniature perfume bottle by David Salazar, which matches one of his paperweight designs (see number 291), sets the moon and stars against a dramatic night sky. $120

364 Reminiscent of the classic Mount Washington plaque, this modern Saint Louis version contains a bouquet of many-petaled red, white and blue clematis-type flowers with complex millefiori stamens set on an opaque white ground. Limited edition, 1984. $700

365 This antique Saint Louis clear wafer dish with an elegant blue and white torsade rim rests on a scrambled millefiori paperweight base. $1200

366 Used by Victorian ladies as handcoolers, these unusual egg-shaped antique Saint Louis paperweights contain dozens of colorful millefiori canes in close packed and scrambled patterns. The second piece from the left is clearly signed SL 1845 at the base in blue letters on a white ground. Prices range from $600 to $1600.

367 Gold foil insects, birds and shamrocks are encased in clear glass over a color ground in these distinctive pieces of jewelry by John Gooderham.

Pierced earrings (bee, bird or butterfly):
Regular:	$60
Single white overlay:	$80
Double blue over white overlay:	$100

Lapel pin or tie tack (swan, shamrock, horse or elephant): $50

368 Handsome millefiori cufflinks, pendant, and lapel pin or tie tack by Saint Louis are available in red, green or blue.

Lapel pin or tie tack:	$90
Pendant:	$100
Cufflinks:	$150

369 This elegant pendant by David Lotton is made of web thread iridescent glass with gold wire fittings. $40

BOOKS
AND
ACCESSORIES

370 Classic French Paperweights This enjoyable and beautifully illustrated book by Edith Mannoni presents a detailed history of paperweight making in France from the discovery of sulphides in 1780 to the present revival of paperweight making by Baccarat and Saint Louis. Originally published in France as *Sulfures et Boules Presse-Papiers,* this 9″ × 12″ book has full-color photographs on every page and extensive captions and information. Hardcover. $35

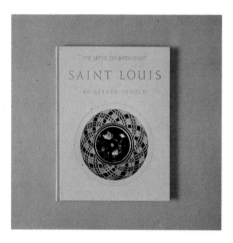

371 The Art of the Paperweight—Saint Louis Written by Gérard Ingold, the commercial director of Cristalleries de Saint Louis, and edited by Lawrence H. Selman and Linda Pope-Selman, this book provides superb photographs and illustrations, and a definitive history of Saint Louis paperweights. It contains rare archival information about the classic period of paperweight making at Saint Louis, as well as a complete full-color catalogue of the company's limited edition paperweights issued from 1970 to 1981. Hardcover. $49.50

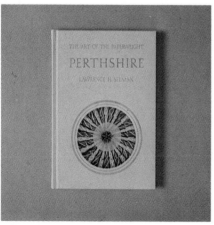

372 The Art of the Paperweight—Perthshire The history and origins of Perthshire Paperweights Ltd. of Scotland, as well as a description of the paperweight making process and a complete color catalogue of the company's weights from 1969 to 1983, are included in this interesting and informative book. Written by Lawrence H. Selman with the cooperation of Perthshire's founder and director, Stuart Drysdale. Hardcover. $34

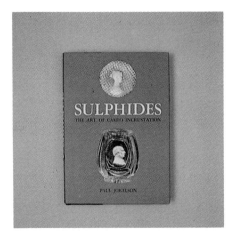

373 Sulphides—The Art of Cameo Incrustation The history of sulphides, one of the oldest and most fascinating of all paperweight styles, is chronicled and explored in this well-researched book by paperweight scholar and historian Paul Jokelson. This hardbound edition comes in a protective slipcase. $15

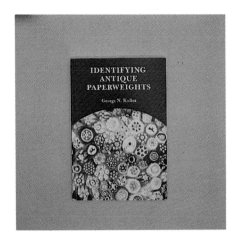

374 Identifying Antique Paperweights This interesting and extremely detailed book, written by George N. Kulles, presents collectors with an excellent guide for identifying nineteenth-century millefiori paperweights produced by the major factories. The book points out subtle differences and distinctions in millefiori canes, patterns and motifs, and overall weight appearance which collectors and connoisseurs will find invaluable. $20

375 Flora in Glass—Paperweights by Paul J. Stankard This exhibition catalogue surveys the work of paperweight artist Paul Stankard from 1971 to 1981. Seventy-one paperweights are illustrated in full color in this hardbound edition. $32.50

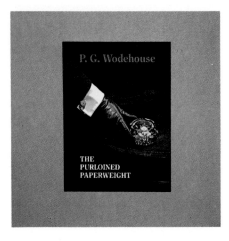

376 The Purloined Paperweight This wonderfully zany novel by P. G. Wodehouse, which revolves around one man's obsession with paperweights, is full of eccentric characters and humorous plot twists. Wodehouse fans and paperweight enthusiasts alike will enjoy this delightful book, which has been out of print since shortly after it was first published in 1967. Hardcover. $14.95

377 Glass Paperweights Millefiori canes and faceting styles of the classic French paperweight making factories are discussed in this informative book by Patricia McCawley. It also includes information and illustrations concerning antique and contemporary paperweight production. Hardcover. $9.95

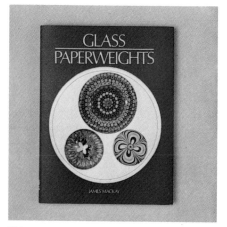

378 Glass Paperweights In this well-written book, author James Mackay presents a concise and informative survey of the history of glass paperweights from their origins to the contemporary revival of the art form. The book has both color and black-and-white plates.
Softcover: $8.95
Hardcover: $15.95

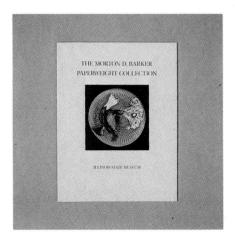

379 The Morton D. Barker Paperweight Collection More than 200 classic paperweights from the remarkable Morton D. Barker collection are described and pictured in this fine catalogue prepared by the Illinois State Museum. $17.50

380 Important Paperweights from the Collection of Paul Jokelson, New York This catalogue was published by Sotheby's of New York in conjunction with the record-breaking sale of Paul Jokelson's paperweight collection in 1983. The elegantly designed book contains large-size, full-color photographs and descriptions of each of the seventy-one weights sold in the auction, including the famous $143,000 Pantin silkworm weight. Hardcover. $40

381 1984 PCA Bulletin Included in this issue: "The Clara S. Peck Collection," by Dwight Lanmon; "Something New in Paperweights—Diatreta and Insculpture"; "How I Took Paul Jokelson to Japan," by Lynne Stair; "Cup and Saucer Sulphide of Henri IV"; "A Bed of Pansies"; "Sulphides: 'The Noble Simplicity and Quiet Grandeur' "; "Important Antique Paperweights"; "The Franklin Schuell Collection of Miniature Paperweights"; "Sulphides—The Art of Cameo Incrustation"; and "A Superb French Collection of Antique Sulphides." $25

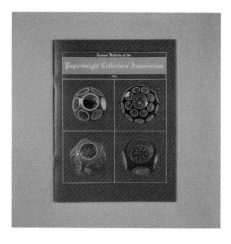

382 1983 PCA Bulletin Articles in this issue include: "An English Garden," about Roy Moore's paperweight collection; "1953–1983—An Amateur Reminisces," by Gérard Ingold; "Collection of a Gentleman"; "Engraved Garland Weights of Debbie Tarsitano and Max Erlacher"; "Hitherto Unpublished 1983 —A Family Affair"; "A Rare Sulphide"; "Always Worth Its Weight"; "Charles Kaziun—Almost Fifty Years in the Business of Glass"; "A Rare Candelabra"; "A Garden of Roses"; and "A Rare Baccarat Tumbler." $20

383 1982 PCA Bulletin The following articles are included in this issue: "In Memory of F. Regnault Fairchild and His Collection of Paperweights"; "A Collection in Beautiful, Balmy Barbados"; "New York/New Jersey State Chapter Paperweight Association Visits the Vandermark/Merritt Glass Studios"; "Hitherto Unpublished 1982," by Theresa Greenblatt; "A Clichy Masterpiece"; "Ayotte's Glasscapes—Painting with Glass"; "An Unrecorded Sulphide Collection"; "Additions to a Collection"; "Visit of Marechal Canrobert at Baccarat on April 21, 1858"; and "The Collection of Dr. Leon Darnis." $20

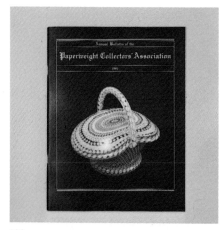

384 1981 PCA Bulletin Included in this *Bulletin*: "A Pantin Discovery," by Dwight P. Lanmon; "The Paperweight Artistry of Victor Trabucco"; "Paperweights in Needlepoint"; "The Martin Kayser Paperweight"; "Convention 1981"; and a description of the book *The Art of the Paperweight—Saint Louis*. $20

385 1980 PCA Bulletin The following articles are included in this edition: "Glasses from the Strauss Collection," by Dwight Lanmon; "Investment Potential of Paperweights," which charts the rising prices in paperweights from 1950 to 1980; " The Beauty of Bacchus"; "The Flame Burns Bright," about the Kontes brothers and their paperweights; and "Whitefriars Then and Now." $20

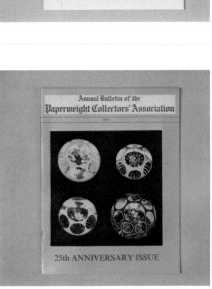

386 1979 PCA Bulletin Highlights of this edition: "French Millefiori Close-Up," with photos of typical Baccarat, Clichy, and Saint Louis canes; "The Crystal Garden," paperweights by Delmo and Debbie Tarsitano; "Birds ... and Rick Ayotte"; "Orient & Flume—Iridescence and Beyond"; and "Paperweight Restoration," by George Kulles. $20

387 1978 PCA Bulletin Featured in this *Bulletin* are: "Our Twenty-Fifth Anniversary," by Paul Jokelson; "The Paperweight Collection of the Hon. Amory Houghton"; "Jewels of Glass from a Captain's Sea Chest," a look at rare weights from a private collection; "Debbie Tarsitano—The Ultimate Challenge"; "Le Rendezvous à Saint Louis," the Selmans' account of their trip to the Saint Louis factory in preparation for the book *The Art of the Paperweight— Saint Louis*. $20

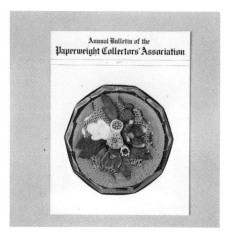

388 1977 PCA Bulletin Articles in this edition of the *Bulletin* include: "Paperweights at Smith College Art Museum," which highlights rare American and French weights; "Homage to Madame Colette," Gerard Ingold's recollections of this famous French collector; "Robert Ray Banford—Paperweight Artisan"; and "New Paul Joseph Stankard Orchids." $20

389 Collectors' Paperweights–Price Guide and Catalogue (1983 edition) Color photographs of more than 300 antique and contemporary glass paperweights and information concerning their design, production and prices are included in this valuable reference which is now out of print. $15

390 Collectors' Paperweights–Price Guide and Catalogue (1981 edition) This price guide contains full-color photographs of more than 200 antique and contemporary paperweights as well as valuable reference information for collectors. Now out of print. $15

391 Jigsaw Puzzle Over 1000 pieces make up this colorful puzzle of antique and contemporary paperweights from the cover of our 1983 catalogue. The puzzle measures 23″ × 29″. $12.50

392 Corning Exhibition Jigsaw Puzzle Forty-two magnificent paperweights are depicted in this jigsaw puzzle designed from an exhibition poster produced by the Corning Museum of Glass. The puzzle has over 600 pieces and measures 18″ × 24″. $12.50

393 Cataloguing Kit; Lucite Stands Excellent for both beginning and experienced collectors, this kit includes printed catalogue cards, self-adhesive labels, an information handbook, and file box. The system is designed to simplify cataloguing and record keeping and provides a complete reference for insurance records and verifications of authenticity. $15

Lucite stands (minimum order: 6 at $2.50 each). $15

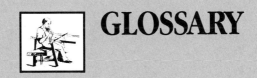

GLOSSARY

GLOSSARY

Air ring An elongated air inclusion encircling a weight near the base, usually above and below a torsade.

Arrow cane A millefiori section made from rods containing a three-pronged arrow motif.

Base The bottom of a paperweight.

Basal ring The ring around the bottom of a concave base where the paperweight comes in contact with the supporting surface.

Basket An outer row of millefiori canes, pulled together underneath the motif to form a staved enclosure for the decorative elements; a latticinio ground pulled down in the center (as in Saint Louis and American fruit weights).

Bouquet A floral design composed of more than one flower.

Cane A molded or bundled glass rod that has been pulled out to miniaturize the interior design.

Carpet ground An overall pattern of identical millefiori canes used as a backdrop for a pattern of other canes or decorative elements.

Chequer weight A paperweight in which the millefiori canes are separated by short lengths of latticinio twists in a checkerboard fashion.

Cinquefoil A garland of canes having five loops.

Clear ground Clear glass used as a background for a paperweight design.

Close concentric millefiori A spacing scheme in millefiori weights with tightly packed concentric circles of canes.

Close packed millefiori A spacing scheme in millefiori weights with a tightly packed random arrangement of canes.

Cog cane A millefiori cane which has been molded with a serrated edge. This type of cane edge is quite common on silhouette canes.

Color ground Opaque or transparent colored glass used as a background for a paperweight design.

Concentric General name for any spacing scheme in millefiori weights with concentric circles of canes placed around a central cane or cluster of canes. Concentric weights are either "open" (circles spaced relatively far apart), "close" (circles close together), or "spaced" (millefiori canes set equal distances apart in vaguely defined concentric circles).

Crown (or dome) The glass in a paperweight which is above the motif.

Cushion Ground on which the decorative element(s) of a paperweight rests. It is usually convex in appearance when viewed through the top or sides of the weight.

Edelweiss cane A white star-shaped millefiori cane with a core of bundled yellow rods.

End-of-day weight See scrambled millefiori.

Facet (or printy) The level or concave surface formed when the side or top of a paperweight is shaped with a flat or rounded grinding wheel. (Printy usually refers to a concave facet.)

Filigree See **lace**.

Flash A thin coating of transparent glass applied to the base of a paperweight, or the entire weight in the case of a flash overlay.

Floret A flower-like pattern within a cane.

Garland A pattern of one or more chains of canes in a millefiori paperweight.

Handcooler An egg-shaped paperweight, once a common accessory for women.

Honeycomb A millefiori cane whose cross-section resembles the cell pattern of a honeycomb.

Initial cane See **signature cane**.

Jasper ground Paperweight background formed by a mixture of two colors of finely ground glass.

Lace (or filigree, muslin, or upset muslin) White or colored glass thread spiraled around a clear rod. Short lengths are used in a jumbled arrangement to form a background for the decorative elements.

Lampwork Manipulation of glass by means of a burner or torch.

Latticinio A lacy backdrop created from white and clear glass. Whereas lace is uniformly chaotic, latticinio is a basketweave pattern. The effect is created by laying white glass rods in a pattern over glass and blowing the mass into a bubble, which is then collapsed.

Magnum A paperweight whose diameter exceeds 3¼ inches.

Making Mark An indentation around a weight where the halves were put together.

Millefiori From the Italian phrase for "a thousand flowers". Used to describe the canes used in many weights.

Muslin See **lace**.

Nosegay A motif consisting of a flat bouquet using millefiori canes as flowers.

Overlay A paperweight that has been coated with one (single overlay), two (double overlay), or three (triple overlay) layers of glass, and has then had windows or facets cut in it to allow visual access to the inner motif. Flash overlays are coated with translucent glass before cutting.

Pastry mold cane A millefiori cane which flares or "skirts" out at its basal end.

Picture cane A silhouette cane employing more than one color within the silhouette.

Piedouche French term for footed weight.

Pinchbeck weight Metallic disk made of a zinc-copper alloy and featuring a design in bas-relief. The disk is covered with a magnifying lens which is then fitted to a pewter or alabaster base.

Printy See **facet**.

Quatrefoil A four-lobed design used as a garland pattern; a faceting scheme.

Ribbon A cane containing a flat ribbon-like element, sometimes twisted, used in crown weights, torsades, and chequer weights.

Rock ground (or sand ground) A granular, uneven paperweight ground formed with unfused sand, mica flakes, and green grass.

Rod A cylindrical length of glass, usually containing a simple molded design of more than one color; the basic component of a millefiori cane.

Scrambled millefiori (or end-of-day weight) A millefiori paperweight design in which whole and broken canes, and sometimes white or colored lace, are jumbled together to fill the weight.

Signature cane A millefiori cane bearing the name or initials of the weight's factory of origin or artist who created it.

Silhouette cane A millefiori cane whose cross section reveals the silhouette of an animal, flower, or human figure.

Star cut A many-pointed star incised into the base of the weight for decoration.

Sulphide A three-dimensional ceramic medallion or portrait plaque used as a decorative enclosure for a paperweight or other glass object.

Torsade An opaque glass thread loosely wound around a filigree core, usually found near the base of a mushroom weight.

Trefoil A garland with three loops.

Twist White or colored glass threads spiraled around a clear glass rod.

Upright bouquet A three-dimensional grouping of canes and stylized lampwork flowers set in a bed of leaves.

Upset muslin See **lace**.

Whorl rod A millefiori cane component with a spiral cross section. Often used as the center of a cluster of star rods.

Window A facet on an overlay paperweight.

PAPERWEIGHT RESTORATION

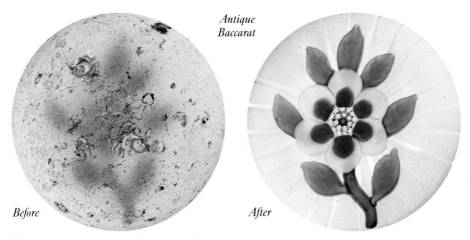

Antique
Baccarat

Before   *After*

DELICATE IMAGES crafted from the beauty and brilliance of glass make the paper-weight a work of art. Few other art forms held in the palm of the hand can rival these shimmering, lustrous objects.

However, time does take its toll. Many antique weights found today do not reflect their original condition. The surface of an antique weight may be bruised, scratched, frosted, or even chipped to the extent that it may seem to have little or no collector value. Through proper restoration, that same weight may reveal its original beauty and artistry.

Paperweight conservation is a delicate process that should be attempted only by qualified specialists. During this process an even layer of glass must be removed from the entire weight. The thickness of this layer depends on the depth of the damage. Workers who are unfamiliar with the characteristics of glass can easily destroy the original shape and optics of a paperweight by creating an uneven surface that distorts the design.

We offer the finest quality paperweight conservation services available. Museums and private collectors alike take advantage of this service, knowing that every considera-tion is given to restore the beauty, brilliance and original artistry of the paperweight. A careful evaluation is done before restoration begins; the collector is notified of the recommended procedure and estimated cost.

Our restoration work is done by conservator and glass artist James Shaw. Since 1978 Shaw's expertise in this field has resulted in the restoration of more than a thousand antique paperweights. Many collectors, museums, paperweight dealers, and artists have benefitted from his sensitive and skilled approach to paperweight conservation. His collaborations with well-known artists such as Paul Stankard have resulted in unique contemporary glass paperweights. Several of Shaw's own cut glass sculpture designs, exhibiting his skill and creativity as both an artist and a craftsman, are offered in this catalogue.

If you have an antique paperweight in need of restoration or a modern weight with scratches or chips, please call or write for more information. We will be happy to help you restore your weight to its original perfection.

CONTEMPORARY SULPHIDES AND GRIDEL ANIMALS

Baccarat

Subject	Number produced	
	Regular	*Overlay*
Elizabeth II Coronation	1492	195
Dwight D. Eisenhower	1389	178
Abraham Lincoln	1291	197
George Washington	1182	200
Winston Churchill	558	81
Thomas Jefferson	594	156
Queen Elizabeth II	–	200
Robert E. Lee	913	137
Benjamin Franklin	414	180
Marquis de Lafayette	744	227
Martin Luther	607	86
Pope Pius XII	2157	284
Sam Rayburn	512	93
John F. Kennedy	3572	308
John F. Kennedy (memorial)	314	–
Pope John XXIII	775	343
Theodore Roosevelt	2359	381
Pierre Laval	160	100
Adlai Stevenson	2595	472
Will Rogers	2517	389
James Monroe	2500	400
Herbert Hoover	2500	400
Eleanor Roosevelt	500	400
Andrew Jackson	2500	400
Woodrow Wilson	2400	400
Harry Truman	2400	400
Napoleon Bonaparte	2400	400
Napoleon Bonaparte (memorial)	100	–
Thomas Paine	2000	400
Mount Rushmore	–	1000
Patrick Henry	1500	400
Elizabeth II Jubilee	500	–
Martin Luther King	500	–
Liberty Bell	1000	–
Evangeline Bergstrom	500	–

Baccarat Gridels

Subject	Date issued
Squirrel	1971–2
Rooster	1971
Elephant	1973
Horse	1973
Swan	1974
Pelican	1974
Hunter	1974
Pheasant	1975
Monkey (black)	1975
Deer (black)	1976
Monkey (white)	1976
Lovebirds	1977
Devil	1977
Stork	1977
Dog	1978
Goat	1978
Bird	1979
Butterfly	1979

The rooster and squirrel were issued in quantities of 1200; each subsequent edition was limited to not more than 350 pieces.

Cristal D'Albret

Subject	Regular	Overlay
	Number produced	
	Regular	*Overlay*
Christopher Columbus	1000	200
Franklin D. Roosevelt	2000	300
John F. & Jacqueline Kennedy	2000	121
King Gustav VI of Sweden	1000	–
John F. & Jacqueline Kennedy	–	300
Leonardo da Vinci	1000	200
Douglas MacArthur	1500	300
Mark Twain	1000	225
Ernest Hemingway	1000	225
Paul Revere	800	200
Albert Schweitzer	1000	200
Prince Charles	1000	200
Moon Astronauts	1000	200
John J. Audubon	1000	225
Jenny Lind	410	170
John Paul Jones	430	170
Charles Lindbergh	400	170
Sitting Bull (terra cotta)	500	–
(tricolor)	500	–
Mahatma Gandhi (terra cotta)	500	–
(tricolor)	500	–
Martin Luther King (tricolor)	325	–
Ronald Reagan	500	300
Prince & Princess of Wales	300	200
Golda Meir	850	150
Begin & Sadat	600	120
David Ben-Gurion	750	150
Moshe Dayan	600	120
Caduceus	1000	–
Scales of Justice	1000	–

Saint Louis

Subject	Regular	Overlay
	Number produced	
	Regular	*Overlay*
Queen Elizabeth II	1226	–
General François Ingold	9	–
Marquis de Lafayette	250	–
King Saint Louis	2000	20
Robert Schuman	300	–
Iranian Monarchy	1000	–
Autun Cathedral	400	–
Charles de Gaulle (as president)	2000	–
Suita Trading Company	500	–
U.S. Eagle	–	400
General de Gaulle (in 1940)	1200	700
Jimmy Carter	500	300
Amour	400	–
Pope John Paul II	1000	300
George Washington on horseback (gold inclusion)	650	400
King Tutankhamen (gold inclusion)	600	–
Mask of Agamemnon (gold inclusion)	400	–

SUGGESTED READING

The following out-of-print books are excellent reference sources, and may be available at your local library. We occasionally obtain copies of these books; please call us to check availability and price.

American Glass Paperweights
by Francis Edgar Smith

American Glass Paperweights and Their Makers
by Jean S. Melvin

Antique French Paperweights
by Paul Jokelson

Antique Glass Paperweights from France
by Patricia K. McCawley

Collectors' Pieces—Paperweights
by John Bedford

The Encyclopedia of Glass Paperweights
by Paul Hollister

A Garland of Weights
by Frank J. Manheim

Glass Paperweights—An Old Craft Revived
by Paul Hollister

Glass Paperweights of the New York Historical Society
by Paul Hollister

Les Presse-Papiers Français de Cristal
by R. Imbert and Y. Amic

One Hundred of the Most Important Paperweights
by Paul Jokelson

Paperweights and Other Glass Curiosities
by E. M. Elville

Paperweights For Collectors
by Lawrence H. Selman and Linda Pope-Selman